HARLEY-DAVIDSON
SPORTSTER

ALLAN GIRDLER
WITH PHOTOGRAPHY BY DAVID DEWHURST

MOTORBOOKS
INTERNATIONAL

First published in 2004 by Motorbooks International, an imprint of MBI Publishing Company, Galtier Plaza, Suite 200, 380 Jackson Street, St. Paul, MN 55101-3885 USA

Motorbooks International titles are also available at discounts in bulk quantity for industrial or sales-promotional use. For details write to Special Sales Manager at Motorbooks International Wholesalers & Distributors, Galtier Plaza, Suite 200, 380 Jackson Street, St. Paul, MN 55101-3885 USA.

ISBN 0-7603-1615-5

Edited by Peter Schletty
Designed by Tom Heffron and Chris Fayers

Cover photo by Jeff Hackett

On the Frontispiece: The XLH Sportster could easily be accessorized into a touring bike. *Jeff Hackett*

On the Title Page: When introduced in 1983, the XR1000 was the fastest street bike Harley had ever built. *Jeff Hackett*

On the Back Cover: (Top) Today the XLCR is prized by collectors. (bottom) The exhaust side of the XR1000 shows the influence of Harley-Davidson's dirt track history.

Printed in China.

CONTENTS

INTRODUCTION

That distinctive eyebrow headlight mount has said "Sportster" for five decades.

No one's ever claimed to have been there when the name burst into being. But the point of this book is that the Sportster of 1957 lives on as the Sportster of 2004, which makes it arguably the longest-lived model in motorcycle history. This history, then, is a success story—perhaps even a series of such. For Harley-Davidson's XL model has reinvented itself again and again, while still remaining true to its heritage. This couldn't have happened if it wasn't for Harley-Davidson's own unique history. Pause here to reflect that H-D is now safely launched on its second century. There was a big party and everyone with a faint interest in motorcycles knows the basics: the Davidson brothers and their pal Bill Harley built an engine for fun, took over their dad's backyard shed, prospered, and then survived and prospered again. It's all in the books.

Playing with Words

The Sportster's history evolves out of a unique culture. For one, everyone in Harley-Davidson has always referred to the firm as The Motor Company, spoken with a reverence that demands you capitalize the initial letters. And The Motor Company has its own language.

Harley-Davidson engines don't, for instance, have crankshafts. Harley engines have roller and needle bearings, and they have flywheels that are pressed onto

Brainstorming, do you think? A bunch of guys are jawboning, there's a new model on the way, and the competition has a knack for names, like Trophy, Gold Star, and Atlas. We here at The Motor Company haven't done much of that, but what if we called it . . . Sportster. Perfect.

Nearly 50 years later, it still is.

crankpins after the connecting rods are assembled. It's lots of pieces but not a crankshaft.

Harley engines don't have distributors, either. A distributor, as seen on classic Indians, collects sparks from a coil and delivers it to this cylinder, then that cylinder. But someone at The Motor Company years ago tidied up the process, creating a set of points that triggers a coil with two outlets, firing both cylinders at once. Wasted spark, it's called, and it's worked for years, so Harley engines have timers.

Where an English engine would have a timing chest, and a domestic V-8 would house its timing gear,

Harley engines have . . . a gearcase. Not a gearbox; that's not the same thing at all. An XL engine has its camshafts in the gearcase, the cavity below the cylinders and outboard of the flywheels, because the space also carried the gears for the oil pump and the ignition and (formerly) the generator and, anyway, the H-D parts book lists the camshafts as cam gears.

. . . and with Numbers

The Motor Company's early engineers began using fractions. So the catalog would list an engine's bore as 3-13/16ths inches. Later, when decimals came into use,

Evel Kneivel, good American that he is, performed some of his famous stunts aboard a modified XLCH.

the fractions were converted, from 13/16ths to 0.812. It's important to note that the rounding off isn't always the same, so sometimes it's 0.813.

And then we got metrics—with millimeters—and more conversions, from a stroke of 3.812 inches to one of 96.8 mm. Again, the figures are rounded off and often get fuzzy. So as we move through history, we'll have dimensions that don't fit (and yes, this is more for winning bets than understanding history), but sometimes it's better to print the fact *and* the legend.

. . . and with Letters

This is pure Harley-Davidson. The very first production motorcycles didn't have any designation at all. The company made its first vehicle in 1903 but didn't use any name or designation. Production is reckoned to have officially begun in 1904, so that year's crop was designated the Model 0 (that's a zero, not an "O"). (Unlike the doomsayers of 1999, H-D's founders realized

that the record—either life, century or millennium—begins with zero, not with one.)

In 1909 there was more than one model, so the catalog had the 5, with battery ignition; the 5A, magneto-fired single; 5B, battery and smaller wheels; 5C, same engine with small wheels and magneto; and 5D, the company's first production V-twin.

From that time on, an initial letter has designated an engine. Next came same-engine options. For example, the J was a 61-cid V-twin, the JD was the same engine enlarged to 74 cid, and the JDH was the 74-cid with two-cam valve actuation.

Since those early days, H-D has used all the letters of the alphabet except for I, O, P, and Y. Some are familiar; the JD and the VL and the FLH are household words (OK, in Harley households). Others are more obscure; M and N were two sizes of commercial van (another bar-bet winner). What matters is there are patterns, with L mostly used for higher compression

The XR-750 came into its own when the aluminum-engined version was introduced.

and H for the improvements that were added after L.

It's also important to understand that the letters were designations, they were not abbreviations. The exception to the rule was that S stood for sidecar gearing, A for models sold to the U.S. Army, and C for the same model sold to the Canadian Army.

. . . and with Policy

Much later in its history, Harley-Davidson would take advantage of the term "evolution."

In fact, H-D made a practice of evolving models one small step at a time. In the time frame used here, Harley's big twins grew from 61 to 74 cid with the same heads, etc. Both versions replaced the iron Knuckleheads with alloy Panheads, then the Panhead suspension changed from leading link to telescopic tubes, followed by a swingarm rear suspension, followed by electric starting, followed by higher-performance Shovelheads, and so on and so forth.

This was planned and done carefully over time. It's important now because it lets us deduce what The Motor Company was doing on its way to designing, introducing and producing the Sportster.

The XR-750 proved so dominant on American dirt tracks that other manufacturers gave up on the genre.

CHAPTER ONE

MEET THE FAMILY

The XRTT used the bulbous, but effective, fairing and rear section first seen on the KTRR.

Above: *Harley-Davidson entered the postwar ear in 1952 with the Model K, a sidevalve 45 cid (now called 750cc) V-Twin. It was unit construction and came with swing arm rear suspension and telescopic forks, plus a hand clutch and foor gearshift, by no coincidence exactly what the improved rivals had to offer. It was handsome but slow.*

When the Allied forces began knocking Axis aircraft out of the skies faster than Japan and Germany could replace planes or pilots, when it was clear who'd win World War II, savvy industrialists began making postwar plans. They knew that when Johnny came marching home he'd have Victory on one arm and Prosperity on the other. That is, the generation that survived the Depression and won the war would be ready to spend money and enjoy it.

Postwar business planners can be divided into two groups; not always in equal proportion, but there was a clear division. The bosses and planners at Ford, General Motors, and Chrysler reckoned the public would buy anything they could get, which gave time for the sellers to tailor the market and take advantage of the war effort's technology. Other planners figured the public would go for the new and different. So Kaiser, Fraser, Studebaker, Crosley, and Tucker took the biggest steps they thought they could manage and, yes, the odds are stacked for effect.

The Indian Motorcycle Co., Harley-Davidson's only remaining rival, took the more radical route. Indian had a new owner, a visionary named Ralph Rogers, who believed the American public would prefer lightweight, more practical, quieter motorcycles. He commissioned new designs and shut down production of the old-line Scouts, despite everything the dealer network could do. The idea, of course, was

valid, just as Powell Crosley was correct in predicting that the general public would someday want small cars. But the timing was wrong, and it killed Indian and Crosley.

Harley-Davidson sided with the more conservative planners, like Ford and GM. So as soon as it could, Harley went back into production with what it made before the war, and now it takes an expert to tell a 1941 Pontiac or Harley FL from the 1946 version.

Harley made one concession. When the war ended, the winners gave themselves permission to rummage around in the losers' garages, so to speak. German firm DKW had a useful little two-stroke single, which BSA took as the basis for its Bantam, and

Harley-Davidson used it to build the Model S, later the Hummer. (Another quaint historical note: the DKW design was also borrowed by Yamaha, better known back then for musical instruments, which used it in its first motorcycle.)

The Sportster's great-great-grandparents, meanwhile, have a long and illustrative history. It's important to note here that one of the canards hurled at Harley-Davidson during the past 40-or-so years is that all they've built is big, old-fashioned, outmoded twins.

Not so. By 1944, 40 years after production officially began, The Motor Company had made singles and twins, in intake-over-exhaust, side-valve and overhead-valve designs. The twins came in Vee, lateral-opposed

The Model K was practical, witness the full fenders fore and aft and came with options like case guards and dual seat, both seen here.

H-D solved the performance shortfall the quick and easy way, enlarging the 750cc K to the 888cc KH and then adding some race tricks. It was labeled KHK, and it matched the imports in power and speed. Bright paint didn't hurt, either.

and fore-and-aft designs. And what they'd learned— the hard way in the case of the singles and opposed twins—was that they were answers to questions the public hadn't asked.

In the late 1920s, first Excelsior (at the time third out of the three American makers), then Indian, and then H-D, came out with 750-cc, OHV V-twins. They were for racing, they weren't widely sold to the general public, and they were tuned for alcohol fuel. They became so popular that the racing bodies had to create a 750 class.

Thus, when Harley's execs decided to bring out a sport model, they went with a 750-cc (known then, of course, as a 45) V-twin, 45-deg included angle, fore-and-aft, just like the older J and JD big twins. The new model, designated D for baseline and DL with higher compression ratios, was contemporary, with rigid rear wheel, leading-link forks, a front brake, and dual head-lights. The D engine was engine and transmission separate but bridged by the primary drive, three speeds forward with hand shift and foot clutch. The only visible novelty was the generator, mounted vertically at

Power wasn't that much less, as Indian had already proved with its side-valve Sport Scout. And the flatheads were quieter, needed less maintenance and were cheaper to build—no small consideration in 1929. The vertical generator was quickly abandoned and in 1932 the 750, with horizontal generator and with many other changes to the cams, oiling system, frame, and so forth, became the R. Other iterations included the RL, the RLS (with sidecar hauler), and the RLD sport model.

Not a Total Loss

Back in the motorcycle engine's teething days, oil was delivered on demand, so to speak. There was an oil tank along with the gas tank, and both were fed to the engine as needed. Because demand could vary, most motorcycles had an auxiliary oil pump for that hill or high-speed dash.

For some reason, the system became known as "total loss." In our environmentally sensitive age, this has come to imply whirling the oil around the crankcase and dumping it on the ground, which it did not do. A roller-bearing engine only needs a few ounces of oil in the crankcase, so the feed-by-need method was adequate in its day.

But when engines could go faster longer, they acquired a dual-stage system, with a pump driven by the engine. The first stage delivered oil to the bearings and bushings under pressure, and the second stage scavenged the crankcase and pumped oil back to a separate tank. It's a better system, which is why virtually all racing engines use dry-sump lubrication to this day. Indian went to the dry sump in the early 1930s and H-D was forced to follow, first with the legendary 1936 Model E Knucklehead.

In 1937, Harley's other engines, the 750s and the side-valve 74s and 80s, were converted to dry sump, so the 750 was re-designated as the W, WL, WLD, and WLDR. The rest of the machine stayed mostly the same, as in rigid rear wheel, foot clutch, and hand

the engine's left front and provoking the Indian crowd (which needed little provocation anyway) to call it the three-cylinder Harley.

But what matters now is that the D engine was a side valve, aka flathead, and it had four one-lobe camshafts sited in an arc directly below the valves in the gearcase to the right of the vee. Why side valve? Because back then no one really knew much about combustion chambers or fuel. So unless you used alcohol the compression ratio was severely limited. The DL's was rated at 5:1, for instance.

Harley-Davidson's race department offered the KHRM for desert and woods racing. Note the high pipes, the solo seat and the pad on the fender, to allow the rider to crouch on the straights.

Next page: *Below the frame tubes is a skid plate, protecting the engine from the unavoidable rocks.*

shift via a lever at the left side of the fuel tank. When World War II broke out, H-D supplied the WLA for the U.S. Army, and the WLC for Canadian forces, and shipped thousands overseas for our allies. They still turn up in Russia, even today.

As previously noted, at the end of the war Harley-Davidson took a cautious approach, putting the W series and the E and F big twins back into production and selling all they could make. In 1947, The Motor Company took a radical step and brought out a two-stroke single, as mentioned earlier. And in 1952, they went contemporary and introduced a

motorcycle version of the Chevrolet Corvette.

When the Western world gained prosperity after the war, the better-off adopted imports, as in MGs and Jaguars and Porsches along with BSAs and Nortons. GM countered by letting Chevrolet offer a sports car. It had side curtains like the Jaguars and MGs, and it used a fiberglass body, the material of the future they thought then, how could it fail? That sleek, streamlined shape covered a dull inline six powering a two-speed automatic, is how it failed. Over at Ford they used the new V-8, but with automatic and mushy suspension, and although the Thunderbird sold, it didn't stop the

imports from winning races and creating a new market.

The parallel is that in 1952 H-D introduced the Model K. It had modern, competitive specs, as in swingarm rear suspension, telescopic front end, foot shift (on the right like the English bikes, and unlike the newly-foot-shift FL.) The engine was unit construction; two-piece cases with four cavities. The flywheels and rods were front and center, with the four-speed transmission directly aft. The left side had the primary drive and clutch (drive side as the Brits say), and the right side was the timing side, with drive for the ignition and oil pump and with the four one-lobe camshafts in an arc below the valves. The valves were in the cylinder's side valves, just like the W, the D, and the R predecessors. And the K was a 45, as we said then, a 750cc engine again like the class of 1929.

Why? First, because in 1952, Ford, Hudson, Packard and their peers were still using side-valve engines. As a matter of fact, Hudson would rule the stock car tracks with theirs. Higher-octane fuels and the higher compression such fuel allowed hadn't gone mass market yet. (Cadillac and Oldsmobile began the revolution in 1949, and Chevrolet took the prize with the mouse-motor V-8 in 1955, but that came later.) But perhaps more important to this history, the American motoring companies didn't understand why the American motoring public wanted Triumphs of two or four wheels.

Back with what they did understand, H-D offered some variations on the K. There was the racing KR, with the basic configuration using a higher compression ratio, hot cams, ball-bearing mains, magneto ignition, and a bigger carb, with rigid rear wheel.

There was also a break in tradition. The tuned street K was designated the KK. H-D practice would have dictated it be the KL, but instead those letters

FUN WITH NUMBERS

All right, the misinformation concerning the specs for the XL and the KH engines is trivial, but it's still fun. It's a good way to win bets and it does finally set the record straight.

The math starts with Harley-Davidson's former habit, shared with most industrial workers at the time, of using fractions. The official book says the W series engine had a bore of 2½ inches and stroke of 3¹³⁄₁₆ inches.

The Model K's bore and stroke are listed as 2.75-inches by 3.8126-inches No change, except maybe from sliderule to calculator. The KH got a stroke of 4⁹⁄₁₆, or 4.5625 inches, and the bore in most places is listed as 2.75-inches, on occasion 2.745 but no one remembers why.

If you use the standard formula, *pi* times the radius squared times stroke times number of cylinders, the models D, W, and K all displace 45.28 cid, rounded off to 45 cid and pronounced "forty-five," not four-five and definitely not 750, which came much later.

Run the KH through the formula and the displacement is 54.19 cid and here's where the confusion begins. Normal practice is to round to the nearest whole number, which gives us 54 cid. The Motor Company, for reasons as plain as they are shaky, rounded up, and the KH always seems to be listed as 55 cid.

The new XL engine had the same configuration as the KH, except for the cylinder heads, and came with a 3-inch bore and went back to the 3.812-inch stroke of the earlier forty-fives. Here, the formula gives us 53.89 cid. Round that one off and it's 54 cid, the same as the KH if it's done honestly. And that's why folks always seem to say the two engines are the same size.

Enter the metric system, and things get worse. Again with the standard formula, 1,000 cc equals 61 cid, and the XL's 53.89 displacement in cubic inches becomes, yes, the 883 cc we've seen for at least a generation.

That's fine and accurate, but there have been those who post-dated the metric application and have claimed the KH was also 883, as in they're both 54 cid, right? Wrong. The formula gives us 54.19 over 61 comes to 888 cc.

And the point? There's no sense doing research if you don't do it right, and you read it here first.

And the Sportster engine isn't a KH engine with new heads.

were used for an experimental OHV 750-cc V-twin that never made it into production. And there was the KRTT, a kit to fit the KT with swingarm rear suspension, front brakes and a bigger fuel tank, for road and TT racing. The K also had a big fuel tank and the KR borrowed the smaller tank from the two-stroke single now called the Hummer. Rules required production parts for AMA racing, but it didn't matter which model the parts came from (and we'll see this tank again!). For even more of a stretch, there was the KRM, an off-road racing machine, with the longer-lived K internals, the hot cams, big carb, straight pipes, and a skid plate for the desert races and scrambles in vogue long before the word "motocross" came into use.

Against all this was the simple fact that the K didn't sell. It wasn't exactly slow, but neither was it fast and sporting. The English bike makers were undeterred and their riders unimpressed.

Just because the slogan "There's No Substitute for Cubic Inches" came from the car guys doesn't mean it's not part of the H-D credo. In 1954, the K engine was given a longer stroke: 4.56 inches from the original 3.81 inches. The nominal displacement became 54 cid rounded off in inches, or 888cc in metric. This was a help, as the 888-cc side-valve could keep up, all else being equal, with the 650-cc imports. And there was the tuned version, the KHK, and a KHR, a KHRTT, and a KHRM, all like the K versions except bigger inside. One major difference was that the early K transmissions broke, and warranty repairs were expensive because the cases had to be split to get at the gears. But in 1955 all KH models got a trapdoor; remove primary and clutch and a couple of bolts and the gears and shafts came out as an assembly, just as all XLs (and all racing motorcycles) still use.

And it's worth noting here that just as the JH was a better version of the J, and the VLH bigger and faster than the VL, so did H designate a step up for the K model. But the KH was just a stopgap. The Motor Company was busy developing the Hydra-Glide, the Duo-Glide, and the shift (get it?) from hand to foot and clutch from foot to hand.

The KH held the fort, which was all it had to do until the first truly postwar, contemporary, competitive Harley-Davidson arrived.

It was, of course, the Sportster.

The KHK kept the dealer showrooms filled until the Motor Company was ready to move into the modern era.

CHAPTER TWO

FIRST COMER

The telescopic front fork was still relatively new technology in 1957, at least for Harley.

The XL Sportster was clearly based on the K series and was just as clearly supposed to be a junior version of the big Harley twins, as illustrated by the full-coverage fenders and generous fuel tank.

Just so we begin on the correct foot, be advised that to call the Sportster a KH converted to overhead valves isn't just wrong, it's exactly wrong. The K and KH were apprentice Sportsters.

Consider Harley-Davidson history and habits. There was never a prejudice *per se* against overhead valves. H-D used OHV engines in racing back in the teens and twenties and saved the company with the OHV Model E in 1936. There were prototype ohv 45-cid V-twins in the 1930s, there was the KL that never went public and a couple of KRs with overhead valves raced in secret in the early 1950s.

Parallel with that, H-D stuck with the rigid rear wheel and leading-link forks when the alloy Panhead replaced the iron Knucklehead, then did telescopic forks, swingarm rear suspension, foot shift and hand clutch with the Panhead engine.

Step by careful step, is the Harley way.

So it made sense to go for unit construction—several years ahead of the English, by the way—and

full suspension and foot shift and so forth, while staying with the reliable, proven and cheap side-valve configuration. Further still, they did it as fast as they could. There was a lot of work for the small engineering department to do, and the big twins were better sellers anyway. So it's not surprising that the really new and modern model didn't arrive until Model Year 1957, that is, late in 1956.

And, in keeping with Milwaukee being close to Detroit, Harley-Davidson wasn't all that far behind;

Ford's OHV V-8 arrived in 1954 and Chevrolet's in 1955.

The Basics

The Sportster's cycle parts, as the English call the frame, suspension, and attachments, really were improved versions of the K and KH. The frame consisted of steel tubing, the backbone, and front and rear downtubes, bridging and locating three iron junctions; a casting for the steering head, forgings for the rear engine mount/swingarm pivot, and the seat/shock

Early XLs came with cast alloy primary covers that had "Sportster" cast into the panel in the center. The covers didn't seal well and they cost extra, so later models came with stamped steel covers.

The XL's second model year brought more power, in the form of the XLH, H meaning a new variation. You can't see the tuning, but you can see this example's front and rear crash guards, the extra lights and the turn signals, yes in 1958.

absorbers mount. The frame is relatively short because the shocks mount beneath the seat at the top and mid swingarm at the bottom. The junction also carried tubes for the seat, a carryover from the big twins. At the lower rear, the cases are located by the junction but there was an alloy mount that fit over the cases and bolted to the junction—and cracked more often than not, but that came later. It all sounds and looks old-fashioned now, but at the time the steel and iron frame was simply the most practical way to get the job done.

The wheels were 18 inches in diameter, front and rear. There may have been some marketing at play here. The K and KH used 19-inch wheels, while the big twins had 18s from the factory, with optional fat 16-inchers (well, five inches was fat back then). There were virtues to all sizes. The taller, thinner wheels and tires gave a better angle of attack on rough roads, of which there were many at the time. The lower, wider wheels and tires gave a more comfortable ride. (Until proven wrong by radical racer Mickey Thompson, science held that tire width didn't add to or subtract from traction, but that's another legend.) The smaller wheels did give lower ride and seat heights, which have always been popular. So the guess here is that the 18s were for looks and comfort. The tires were conventional crossply, and the wheels were built-up wire or spoke wheels. Again, like all the normal motorcycles of the day.

Brakes were drum, 8-inch-diameter, leading and trailing shoes, one inch across, front and rear. Again, this was standard stuff, as disc brakes were just beginning to appear on racing cars and wouldn't get to bikes for another generation.

One difference worth noting here was that the Sportster's rear sprocket was riveted to the brake drum. This surely made it vibration-proof, but also meant machine shop time when the sprocket wore. And that final drive gearing could only be varied at the output sprocket. Not a problem, either one, but it was different.

Sportster suspension was also state of the art, which means how everyone does it, and don't let the TV guys tell you otherwise. H-D had some experience with telescopic forks and swingarm rear hubs by this time. Both front and rear used coil springs, and damping by hydraulic fluid. The rear shocks came with covers, while the fork tubes had rubber boots. This made them water- and dirt-proof, and was one of the few places where the new Harley looked a lot like its rivals from abroad.

The Engine

This is where the "New" begins.

The configuration was familiar; that is, unit construction, engine, and gearbox in one unit. There were the four cavities as seen in the K models, with flywheels front and center, gearbox directly after, primary drive on the left, and timing on the right.

Dimensional confusions are cited elsewhere in this chapter, but the point is the XL engine wasn't exactly the same displacement as the KH engine, and the displacement was achieved through literally different dimensions.

Smallish speedometer fits in nacelle that carries the headlight, with warning lights in the headlight itself. The red knob controls a steering damper (and the knob itself is a prank, borrowed from someplace else and no, this XLH has not been restored.)

The 3-inch bore was new. The 3.81-inch stroke was a repeat of the original K's measurements. The larger bore and shorter stroke followed the practice of the day: a shorter stroke allowed higher engine speeds and the larger bore gave room for bigger valves to take advantage of the higher revs, which multiplied the benefit of better breathing. Neat, eh?

Some of the details were pretty much carryover, such as the generator at the front of the cases driven by the gears working the four one-lobe camshafts, with the ignition timer atop the gearcase (Harleyspeak for the timing case 'cause the camshafts are called cam gears) and the two-stage oil pump below the case.

The clutch was dry (well, it was supposed to be, but that comes later), inside the clutch hub, and covered to keep out the gear oil shared by the transmission and primary drive. And, as mentioned, the gears were on two shafts, removed in unit by unbolting the trapdoor behind the clutch.

The upper end, the cylinders, cylinder heads, and rocker boxes, were new. Again, they were contemporary in that the combustion chamber formed half a sphere, a hemisphere as seen in Chrysler's fabled Hemi V-8. The pistons were domed, that being the easiest way to vary compression ratio. Working through roller tappets, the cams pushed rods up through spring-loaded covers, to the rocker arms mounted in boxes, assemblies atop the heads proper. The rocker boxes were aluminum; the cylinders and heads were heavy cast iron.

Because this was remarked upon and even criticized generations later, it's worth noting that back then there was no comment, nor did anyone fault Ford or Chevrolet for their iron blocks and heads. Iron is cheap, workable, plentiful and strong. 'Course, there is the fact that aluminum sheds heat quicker and more efficiently than iron. And the fact that a water-cooled engine, as in Ford and Chevy, comes with an even more efficient way to stay cool.

Harley-Davidson had experience with alloy. Several years before this the iron Knuckleheads were replaced by alloy Panheads, never mind that the experimental KL, done at the same time, used alloy for its heads and barrels.

Journalist Buzz Buzelli, who worked for The Motor Company early in his career, has written that the alloy KL was dropped in favor of the iron XL because the XL engine was less work, would take less time to develop, and needed to get the machine on the market soonest. That makes sense. It's also common gossip that aluminum is more demanding, takes more time and effort at the foundry, a lesson H-D learned when the Panhead engine had problems when first introduced. The iron XL components weren't any trouble then or later. When the Panheads gave way to the Shovelheads, a design very much like the Sportster's except the Shovel was done in aluminum, it simply showed The Motor Company marching, and not for the first time, to its own drum.

The Designation

The Sportster's name was, of course, made in heaven, while the new model's designation, the code letter (or letters) used by the factory and later the public, are still something of a puzzle.

The tractor-style solo seat provided all-day comfort for the rider of an XLH.

Doubly so.

First, there was the use of a letter already in use. Harley-Davidson had made a practice of one letter per engine, as in the J for the plain old V-twin, D for the side-valve middleweight, E for the 61 Knucklehead, even F when the 61 grew to 74 cid.

And we've seen how the second letters have been used, with L for a first stage of tune from the original, H for higher tune or more displacement. The V was the plain side-valve 74, the VL was tuned, the VLH was the tuned side valve enlarged to 80 cid, and so forth.

So here, in the fall of 1956, Harley-Davidson announced the Sportster and it was designated XL.

Harley's first X was the BMW copy, a side-valve boxer twin, made for the U.S. military when the real BMW was starring (for the German army, of course) in the Middle East. And because there was a limited production run for our army, it was always known as the XA.

Why the repeat? As we've seen, there are a couple of letters H-D hasn't done much with. Why not, oh, M or T? But they didn't, and no one in the know has ever said why.

We can make a better guess with that second letter. There were early prototype OHV engines, remember, and higher compression was still something of a

The overhead-valve XL represented a great leap in power over the old sidevalve KH.

mystery then. One of those early OHV twins ran a compression ratio of 6.8:1. Whuddaya bet that was the plain version and that it did so well in the tests they popped the compression ratio to 7.5:1 and it worked fine, so they put the tuned version, the XL, into production from the first?

The Product

A mild warning here: The detailed, accurate, and objective test was introduced to the U.S. by John Bond's *Road & Track*. The impartial testing of motorcycles didn't get here until Joe Parkhurst, an *R&T* graduate, founded *Cycle World* in 1962.

Not only that, but Harley-Davidson was never keen on using figures, especially not if they might reflect badly on the product.

What this means for those early days is that the judgments seldom are very, um, judgmental. The magazine guys 50 years ago were members of the same insular family as the factory guys. And the magazines

seldom, as the English said under the same circumstances, met a motorcycle they didn't like. So the factory's first ads for the Sportster refer to "all-new OHV power," "rider-controlled" spark advance, "mellow-sounding" muffler, "comfortable" saddle, and so forth, through 40 features, with the brakes and generator output as the only figures listed.

The first test, in the March 1957 issue of *Cycle*, tells us that the XL has a shorter wheelbase than the KH (57 inches, we'll learn later), the compression ratio was 7.5:1, and the tires were 3.50 x 18 inches. There were estimates then that the engine output was 40 bhp, compared with 38 bhp claimed for the KHK.

Cycle did have honest clocks and tape measures, and they did record fuel use. So we also know the original XL topped out at 101.40 mph, did the standing-start quarter mile in 15.03 seconds and returned 57 mpg during the test.

A general comment about all the motomags—now and then—is that it's interesting to see how the

figures change more than the words do. The 1957 test claims that the Sportster "provides terrific acceleration throughout the speed range and is perhaps the most flexible motorcycle in production today . . . the power comes on instantly and smoothly." Nowadays, when scooters turn in 15 second quarter-mile times and 600-cc sportbikes run through the quarter mile in 10 seconds, the early XL is more notable for its vibration than for its fire-breathing performance. Never mind, the magazine was impressed and said so. Using even better hindsight, note that the *Cycle* test decided the Sportster "is designed primarily for the touring motorcyclist."

Were things different then? It's not that so much, and it's not that the sales guys in Milwaukee didn't yet get it. Instead, Milwaukee was still close to Detroit. At the time, the big Buick had just taken third in sales from the small Plymouth. Big might not have been better, but big sold better, while GM had become the world's largest corporation by persuading the market

that a Chevrolet was a bargain Buick, and a Buick was what you bought until you could spring for a Cadillac.

Now, look again at the '57 XL. Along with the preceding KH, the XL has generously valanced fenders front and back, to shield the rider from the weather. There's a big fuel tank (4.4 gallons, in the catalog, with a 4.1-gallon claimed by *Cycle*: They probably didn't include reserve). It has a car-sized headlight mounted in its own sculpted holder. The muffler is large and quiet, the case guards—"crash bars" until the lawyers took over—are standard. Options included a double seat, a big windshield, and saddlebags.

The Sportster clearly was supposed to be a junior FL, a comfortable mount for the open road, rain or shine. This wasn't a mistake. The marketing guys had in fact picked a niche that *was* a niche.

But what will matter in the years (and chapters) to come, is the proof that The Motor Company had the ability, all too rare in this confused world, to take *Yes* for an answer.

CHAPTER THREE

PERFORMANCE RULES

The XLR engine looks like an XL, but has different cylinder heads and internals.

The XLR (this is a '62, out of time sequence) used a souped XL engine.

How Harley-Davidson took *Yes* for an answer starts with the unquestionable success of the original Sportster. The official data book compiled by Rick Conner says the factory produced (and the dealers presumably sold) 1,983 XLs, plus 418 sold to the U.S. Army and coded XLA in case one turns up in a barn someplace.

Model year 1956 shows 714 KHKs and 539 KKHs, so the move and investment paid off right from the get-go.

But much more was on the way. Some of this history was frankly obscure but, at the same time, one of these four variations changed motorcycling's world, and for the better.

The XLR

The drive here was racing. Back when the Great Depression persuaded the American Motorcyclist Association to award national titles to production bikes, the rules allowed 45-cid side-valve or 30.50-cid

(aka 500-cc) overhead-valve engines. This was done because Harley and Indian were the only two American makers and their sporting models were side valve 45s, while the lone importer then offered 500-cc sports machines from England.

By happy coincidence, the lone importer, Reggie Pink by name, also invented TT racing in America, and named it TT because he thought roaring around an orchard on a stripped road bike was something like racing in the classic Tourist Trophy on the Isle of Man.

It may well have been similar, but for us what matters is that TT was conceived as Sunday sport, for guys who'd ride into the country, remove lights and luggage, get serious air over the jumps, put the stuff back on the bike, and ride home. And because some enthusiasts rode big twins, Harley VLs, and Indian Chiefs, the AMA rules for TT included an open class, i.e., race what ya rode here on. That, in turn, led to Harley-Davidson building and certifying the KHR-TT, a stroked KR engine mostly, with swingarm rear

The XLR was a natural open-class TT racer.

The cylinders are cast iron painted silver and the magneto has replaced the generator in front of the engine's vee.

suspension and brakes, along with the KR dirt tracker and the KR-TT road racer.

There came a crunch in 1957, part of the XL program. By then the side valve was obsolete and so to a degree was the 500-cc sporting twin, as the English moved into 650s. Triumph, BSA, Norton, and others simply kept the 500s in the catalog.

It wasn't that simple for Harley-Davidson, as a 500-cc Sportster made no sense at all. And they'd learned the hard way that the Harley buyer wasn't keen on singles. So H-D management decided to keep the KR in production for dirt track and the KR-TT for road rac-

ing, and told the engineering and racing departments to build a TT contender, to do for the XL what the KHR-TT had done for the KH.

No prize for guessing that the new model was designated XLR, just as R had meant racing in the Harley shop since the WR of 1941.

This was an interesting project. Vintage tuner Jim Carpenter says the only sure way to distinguish a KR or XLR frame from a K or KL frame is to weigh two examples. The R frames used better grade steel tubing, so the walls are thinner and there's less material. So the lighter one should be the R. And the R frames

have the cast steering head a bit higher on the tubes, so the engine is lower.

The XLR came with the swingarm and shocks from the road version, along with drum brakes and telescopic forks. The gas tank was—classic to come!—the peanut tank the KR borrowed from the little two-stroke Hummer. There was no front fender and the rear fender was cut short, again like the KR and not like the XL.

XLR cases looked exactly like XL cases, but used a KR-style engine sprocket, and a quarter-speed oil pump. XLR cams were all new, and they were carried

on ball bearings instead of needle bearings and bushings like the XL or the K engines.

The main bearings were also ball for reduced friction, even though bearing life was measured in hours or races instead of thousands of miles. Because the K, KR, XL, and XLR shared the 3.812-inch stroke, the XLR shared beefed-up connecting rods with the KR. Ignition, again like the KR, was magneto, mounted up front where the road bikes had their generators.

The major difference was the cylinder heads. For the XLR, compression ratio was bumped to 9:1, and the heads got larger valves. They also were made from

Cosmetically the sidevalve KR racer's peanut tank and low dual straight pipes distinguished the XLR from pedestrian XL models.

a new casting, with the most obvious difference being an extended boss for the spark plug, which had 3/4-inch reach. The XL heads have recessed plug holes, and use 1/2-inch plug reach.

The XLR came with dirt track, semi-knob tires, legal in TT but not much use off-road. As sold, a stock XLR weighed 350 pounds dry, and while there were claims of 55 bhp, as fitted with two straight pipes again like a KR, the guess now is 50 horses, tops.

Just considered as itself, as a distinct model, the XLR didn't make much of a splash. The data book shows 26 XLR-TTs produced in the 1958 model year, five in '59, and then the designation disappears from the charts. Much later, the race shop guys will guess perhaps 500 XLRs were built between 1958 and 1971, when for reasons lost in time several of the beasts were assembled for some very insistent customers.

The XLH

Serendipity, which is Greek for happy accident, must have played a big part here.

Either as a result of the XLR research, or work done in parallel on the XL, the engineers learned that

A TT racer needs to be lean and mean, and anything that adds weight without contributing to performance must go.

the Sportster engine was so strong it could easily accept a higher compression ratio than the second-stage XL was given.

High compression is free power, as the extra squeeze gives more efficiency. The engine is stronger and gets better fuel economy, while other changes—camshaft timing or a bigger carburetor—add at some speeds and subtract at others.

The H-D researchers re-did the XL heads, with larger ports and valves, and raised the piston domes. Both were duplications of the XLR tuning, except that for some reason the street engine kept the short-reach plugs and has the recessed plug boss.

This was an engine tune, nothing else. In tune, so to speak, with the earlier JH, the 1920s engine with two camshafts, the 1935 VLH side-valve twin with more displacement than the VL, and the change from FL to FLH when the Panhead big twin got more power; the third stage of tune for the Sportster 883 engine was named XLH. (This sounds fussy here, but there's a reason for the details.)

Further, because the H specs were a stage, cylinder heads that could be used on any XL engine, the XLH appeared as just that, an engine option with the same carb, exhaust, ignition, and so forth as was used on the XL. Every detail looked the same, except for an "H" decal on the oil tank. (The plain and the H models were so alike the factory's photo studio used to shoot the catalog pics minus decal, then with decal, to save time and film.)

The XLC

Here's where the controversy begins and the notes come in handy.

Harley-Davidsons have been ridden off-road since before there was such a thing, since in pavement terms the whole planet was off-road. Competitors like Dot Robinson won enduros in the 1930s and the Hummers, K-models, and even big twins, won class and overall in the legendary Jackpine enduro. But the off-road models didn't do well. The KRM and KHRM mentioned earlier were outclassed by the English twins. Sales weren't just dismal, they were nonexistent.

Another H-D tradition, thank goodness, was the close relationship between the factory and the dealer network. Motor Company history is studded with examples of dealers like Tom Sifton, who could see and correct a flaw the designers had overlooked. They did not always like to admit it, but the execs could take good advice when they got it.

On the occasion that concerns us here, California dealers Sam Arena and Armando Magri said years later that when the Sportster was being planned—and the project wasn't terribly secret—they and some other guys urged the factory to offer a stripped version, not exactly an enduro bike, but something for the sports riders to use in the woods and desert and classics like the Catalina GP.

This rings true. H-D for generations had built to demand, what economists call a pull system. That is, they'd ask the dealers to place orders, so many FLs, so many Servi-cars, so many Hummers, and the factory would build what the dealers could sell. (Years later the big importers used a push system: They'd fill the wharves with unsold bikes and tell the dealers, sell 'em or else.)

Back to this case, Magri said the factory guys agreed to offer the stripped models, provided he and the other Californians would order 60 examples, right then and there, which they did.

The result was a perfect mix and match. The planners used the XL frame, suspension, brakes, and engine straight from the stock XL. They swapped for the XLR's rear fender, peanut tank, magneto ignition, and the two straight pipes routed low down the right side, like the XLR and the KR. There was one option: lights and license plate bracket were offered for an extra $60. Even so, this stripper model was a gamble, a bet against motorcycling's more recent history.

Here's the reason for the notes: When the stripper appeared for model year 1958, it was designated the XLC. The XL is obvious. The C is unexplained.

It doesn't fit H-D practice, for one thing. The KH was followed by the XL, the KR by the XLR, so the rules say the KHRM should have been followed by the XLM, but it wasn't.

Magri and Arena always believed the C was in honor of California, the target market and the source for the idea and the financial support. Nine years later, *The Enthusiast*, Harley-Davidson's in-house magazine, published a history of Sportster engineering and confirmed the legend of the dealers and their support, but said nothing about the third letter. (The magazine seldom gave away any inside facts in any case.)

The front brake on the XLR Sportster.

Beginning in 1959 XLCH came with the now-classic small headlight and eyebrow mount. Allan Girdler

The Legend Begins

When the ads for the 1958 Harley lineup appeared, the Sportster was prominent and there were four, yes four, variations on the new theme.

There was the XL, just as it first appeared except for minor items like new seals to keep the clutch dry inside the wet primary case.

There was the XLH, identical from every angle to the XL but with the higher compression ratio, larger valves, and more power.

There was the XLC, stripped of lights and mufflers and with the smaller tank.

And there was the XLCH, being just what you'd guess, the XLC fitted with the H state of tune.

All these changes and options hint that the variations weren't all conceived after the Sportster was shown to the public. Even so, it was a lot of new stuff for a company as methodical as H-D.

There's an evidence gap here. Conner's records show 579 plain XLs produced for 1958, 711 XLHs (there's a forecast of things to come), 239 XLCHs . . . and no XLCs at all (not on the record, anyway).

Off the record, talking with guys who were there, the legend is that only a handful of the plain strippers were made or sold. That makes sense. Why buy a sport model with less than all the sport you can get?

Management was taking notes. The low-compression models, for on road or off, were quietly dropped. Moreover, the engine with the 9:1 compression ratio and the larger valves became the stock engine. Just as sensibly, the XLCH was equipped for registration, even if the marginal mufflers made street legality a subject for roadside debate.

The 1959 Sportsters, then, came only in two version. (We'll clear the record here and say the XLR was never exactly a Sportster, a point owners then and now will make with some force.)

Marketing played a hand. One of the styling features of that day was that high exhaust pipes gave more ground clearance. So off-road machines had high pipes, leading to high pipes being a signal for trail bike, enduro bike, or whatever your neighbor thought yours was. The 1959 XLCH introduced a small, ineffective muffler, mounted high on the right, fed by two high pipes with a heat shield protecting the rider's leg.

The other visible new introduction was a headlight, as small as state laws allowed, mounted with an eyebrow sort of casting on the top triple clamp.

Not visibly, but perhaps as important, the '59 XLCH came with hot camshafts. The designation was P, and the timing came from the XLR, which used the specs from day one. But they weren't the same cams—well, they were the same cam lobes and the same gears, but the shafts were different. The XLR used ball bearings to carry the shafts, while the XL engine had roller bearings and bushings. P cams for the XLR engine had thin shafts, while the XLCH's P cams had thick shafts. That's why the parts book has two sets of numbers for the same set of lobes and gears.

The Superbike
Starts Here

All these facts are useful, but the important news arrived in 1960, in (of all places) *Hot Rod* magazine.

Or perhaps that wasn't so surprising. Then, as now, gearheads and performance buffs had no problem liking both cars and bikes. *Hot Rod*'s Bob Greene was a motorcycle enthusiast, and a racer, and a gearhead; if Magri and Arena had made a model of the guy they thought would buy a stripped Sportster, that model would have come out like Bob Greene.

In the April 1960 issue of *Hot Rod*, Greene described the XLCH as "Two-wheel hot rodding with a capital "H" in a 55(cq)-cubic inch V-twin that gallops through the standing quarter-mile at over the century mark, explodes up a knee-deep sandwash like it was shot from a gun, and purrs down Main Street with the docility of a scooter. Here are the unwashed facts gained from a two-month, 1,000-mile flogging given the Sampson of sports motorcycles, the hot rod from Milwaukee."

It was some test. Greene and his peers rode around town and cross country, and took the test bike to the drags, and even competed in the Big Bear Run, a cross-desert event that at the time was the largest race in the world.

By the numbers, the '60 XLCH with optional large fuel tank and solo seat weighed 492 pounds, tanks topped off. H-D put the bike's power at 52 bhp, but Greene reported that dyno tests more often showed 55 bhp, or more than one horse per cubic inch. At the drags, the stock Sportster turned an ET of 14.17 seconds with a trap speed of 93.55 mph. A prepped XLCH turned in the thirteens, at 101 mph.

They took off the road gear and swapped for a smaller output sprocket and raced across the desert. They didn't win. In fact Greene dumped his mount and filled the air cleaner with sand and spent half an hour getting the engine going, which to his credit was announced in the test.

Greene also noted that a cold XLCH engine needed some healthy kicks, while the only factual claim that can now be questioned was saying oil use was negligible, the only time in 40 years that was said about the iron XL.

There *is* a word quibble. Greene called the test bike "the Competition Hot job" (formal for CH). He made that up. He didn't say so, but he did. As noted earlier, H by then had been an H-D designation for 40 years, and had nothing to do with hot, while C just sort of popped up.

But then a writer at Harley's ad agency picked up the quote and used it in an ad. So The Motor Company's official history, done by a guy who wasn't there when the CH appeared, assumed the ad was correct and put the claim in the official record, and like the business about how the bee can't fly and you can see the Great Wall of China from out in space, there are still Sportster stories in which Competition Hot gets mentioned and CH never stood for that, never ever, OK?

But that's purist's quibble.

More important here was how the XLCH was recognized at the time. One of *Cycle World*'s first tests, for the October 1962 issue, was a '62 XLCH. The test recalled H-D's long history and said that at the "big" end of the model line (their quotation marks) Harley offered performance, "in the form of a big V-twin engined bike called the XLCH. One's first impression is apt to be that there sure is a lot of it."

This is the context factor, eh? And in 1952, when the U.S. was just meeting the nice people on little Hondas, there was a market for 50 or 90-cc step-throughs. Furthermore, a 250 single was a man's machine, and an 883-cc twin with a wet weight of 480 pounds really was a big motorcycle. Remember, the FL Harleys were so much bigger that they were in a class by themselves.

CW's test XLCH came, they said, in "semi go-to-the-races form," with the little headlight and short dual mufflers, and an optional dual seat and tachometer.

The XLR, fitted here with a big XLH tank for longer events, was a winning machine in open class TT races.

Cycle World was busy earning a reputation for honesty and reported that although the factory claimed 55 bhp (no rpm specified), and that it would deliver one-bhp-per-cubic inch (popularized by Chevrolet five years earlier), "The performance indicates an output nearer 40 bhp than the claimed 55," *Cycle World* wrote. "In England, the Sportster is advertised as having 47 bhp at 5,000 rpm, which seems a trifle conservative . . . we would guess our test bike had about 50 bhp with a peaking speed of 5,500 rpm."

The testers added that all the factories fudged at that time and, anyway, the XLCH "is clearly the fastest mass-produced motorcycle we have had."

How fast was that? The quarter-mile in 14.3 seconds, which lines up with *Hot Rod*'s test, an average top speed of 122 mph (no notes on how they did that test), and a range of 40-60 mpg. The bottom line? "The fastest thing an expert rider is likely to find for sale."

As a parallel if not comparison, *Cycle World* tested an XLH in 1965 and gave it faint praise. The mag said that the "touring" (again, their quote) XLH is "quite a comfortable motorcycle . . . reasonably smooth . . . we were bothered by a tendency for bits under the bike to begin scuffing the pavement at surprisingly moderate angles of lean."

The quarter-mile time was 15.5 seconds, top speed was 98 mph, test weight was 505 pounds (!), and the testers wondered if their machine wasn't a poor example of its type.

Surely sounds like it. But what counts for us here is that the XLH was for touring, the CH for performance, and that was about to become really important, even as modest sales boomed. By the mid 1960s, the arrival of the imports had exposed just about all American boys to the lure of motorcycling.

To pick one excellent example, a California truck driver named Carl Morrow learned to ride on a pal's little machine and liked it so much he got one for himself. It didn't take long before he wanted more speed. He got an English 750 twin, which lost street races, so he got an XLCH and won on the street but lost at the strip. So he began souping up the engine.

Morrow had an advantage, in that Tom Sifton was a family friend and Morrow used to chauffeur Sifton around. The legendary tuner didn't give away any secrets, but Morrow could watch and learn—and he did.

Why the drags? Morrow went to the TT and half-mile races at fabled Ascot. The riders weighed less than he did, and they spent lots of time climbing out of the hay bales, sometimes slowly. Morrow figured it was no

place for a family man, so he ran the drags three times a week, and won.

Why Sportsters? The imports didn't have the muscle, he says now, while improving XL engines was rewarding because "they needed a lot of help."

How so? One factor was the rear engine mount, which cracked when it appeared in 1957 and was still vulnerable when the factory replaced it in 1982. Meanwhile, drag racers, notably the Pingel family, quickly came up with a better mount. (Still available, if you're restoring an XL). The rear of the right case half cracked because that was where the speedo drive gear was. Too much torque would twist the corner off, again something that could and can be fixed.

More to the point, Morrow found the XL stronger than the bigger Harley twins and bigger than the imports and more adaptable that either: His street engine, the one he ran three times a week, used KH flywheels and was bored to 74, then 80 cid, with Dykes cylinders. Then they tried nitromethane and elapsed times dropped into the nines, which is when Morrow "was building faster than I wanted to ride," so he signed rider Ron Finger and won the NHRA nationals three years running with a stock frame and against the imported triples and fours.

Morrow teamed with Leo Payne, also a Sportster tuner. Using a road race fairing from Harley's XRTT (more about that later) they turned 202.379 mph at the Bonneville salt flats, the first conventional—as opposed to laydown streamliner—to top 200.

They took the fairing off and turned 187.

They weren't alone. Anyone who could read or stand on the street corner with his ears open knew the XLCH was the way to go fast. Warner Riley set records at Bonneville, Lance Weil took an XLR engine in a road race frame and won payment races in England.

The factory got into the act, thanks in no small part to the resemblance of the full race XLR to the street racer XLCH. Tuner Dennis Manning built a streamliner and H-D racing supplied an XLR engine

A true desert sled, witness the skidplate beneath the engine, this KRHM has oversize shocks, lightweightforks, plus high pipes and case guards for when, not if, the crash occurs.

whomped to 90 cid and burning nitro, and loaned road race legend Cal Rayborn to the project.

Pause while serious fans get their tapes of *On Any Sunday*, Bruce Brown's evergreen tribute and the best motorcycle movie ever made. OK, it's funny when Rayborn has to learn how not to tip over, but at the

end of the day, the streamliner turned 265.492 mph and held the world record for motorcycles.

Another facet came in AMA nationals. For reasons detailed earlier, the TT classes (plural) were 750 cc or open, later 900 cc. This meant that in the 1930s guys with big twins could race for fun.

What it meant during the iron Sportster era was that Jim Belland and Mert Lawwill (again see *On Any Sunday*) could legally build a special lightweight frame and soup up an XLR engine to 90 bhp while still 883 cc.

The best of several examples was nicknamed "Goliath." It weighed 309 pounds and in the hands of Mark Brelsford, AMA #1 in 1972, was nearly unbeatable. And if it didn't actually have many Sportster parts—clutch plates are the only ones that come to mind right away— it still looked and sounded like what the fans rode in on, which is what counted.

But for the true core of the XLCH legend, we go to Cook Neilson, who's best known as the editor of *Cycle* when that magazine was at its peak, and for winning, the inaugural Superbike race at Daytona's Bike Week on a Phil Schilling-tuned Ducati.

But when asked by *Cycle World* in June 1988 about his favorite motorcycle, Neilson cited his 1964 XLCH.

He used his XLCH to get suspended from college, demoted in the military, carry on his rounds of door-to-door sales attempts, commute to see his girlfriend, set records at Bonneville and the drags, and get into four serious crashes, "only three of which were my fault."

"Through it all, my CH was an indictable co-conspirator and unsavory influence, chuffing happily or exploding enthusiastically . . . we went everywhere and did everything, and at the end of the day, even though we had put a few dings and scratches on each other, my love for that bike was undiminished."

Morrow, Neilson and the other members of the XLCH tribe (or circus) benefited from timing . . . or perhaps their very success brought the limit to their exploits.

The Peak

The best Sportster of all time is tough to pinpoint. There are those who'll say that the very first XLCHs were the best, for instance.

But a better case can be made for the 1966-68 XLCH. In terms of the actual machine, 1966 was the first year for the still-with-us Hamcan air cleaner, a shape as familiar and durable as the peanut gas tank. Behind the air cleaner was a new carburetor, supplied by Tillotson and featuring a diaphragm doing the job formerly done by the float bowl. There was some optional juggling of camshafts, with the choice of full XLR timing for power, or a milder exhaust camshaft (rear cylinder only) for easier starts. The high single muffler had been abandoned because everyone preferred the KR-style short duals, another trademark for XLs. Claimed power was 60 bhp at the brochure, and it wasn't too far off: *Cycle World* tested an XLCH with Linkert carb and got 14.3 seconds in the quarter, while *Cycle*'s Tillotson version was clocked at 14.1 seconds.

It's worth noting that starting early Sportsters was always a technique and/or a challenge. Tests of the day always said you had to learn the drill and then it was easy (and former XLCH owners always said they had it down pat). Neilson, though, recalls a start from cold could sometimes take an hour, and there's no current owner who won't admit that he's done the jacket-off, bump-start routine before and expects to do it again.

Another reason the '66-67 XLCH sets the standard was that this raucous behavior, this challenge to one's talents and expertise, was part of the charm. (Probably still is.)

Furthermore—and perhaps the clincher—during this period the XLCH was not merely the most powerful and fastest production machine on the market, it was as far from its sibling XLH as it could get.

Yes, the buyer could order the shorty duals, peanut tank, and solo seat for the plain H model, or the larger tank for the CH, but most guys didn't. There was a clear distinction between the two, as clear as the gap between XLH and FLH, so the sports version ruled the roost.

But while the Superbike stood tall, the world made a tectonic shift.

CHAPTER FOUR

INTO THE MAINSTREAM

Now we've got some history: This is a 1966 XLCH,
with the low single pipes borrowed from the XLR and the hamcan air cleaner,

Electric start appeared first on the XLH, in the form of the round chromed starter motor between the rear cylinder and the rear exhaust pipe. The addition required new cases.
Jeff Hackett

Novelist Milan Kundera has mused that it's really unfair, having only one life per person. There are so many options, he wrote, it's a shame we'll never know what would have happened if, say, we'd taken the road more traveled, or not run off to join the circus, or, well, made any of the choices we didn't make.

Which is to say, suppose Indian Motocycle (that's how they spelled it, speaking of choices) had perfected the electric start they introduced in 1914? Yes, 1914. When the batteries of 1914 weren't up to the job, Indian chose to abandon the project and for the next 45 years everyone knew electric start would never work.

Mr. Honda hadn't read the book. He presented the Electric Leg as a matter of routine. And while the Yankee, Brit, Italian, and German makers blustered

The small gas tank made for a comfortably narrow motorcycle, with speedometer and tachometer mounted high and visible.

The stamped primary cover on the XLCH has twice as many mounting bolts than the cast one did, and it leaks less.

and evoked tradition and skill, they knew deep down they'd have to follow the market leader.

Harley-Davidson did so in 1964 with the Servi-Car (you could look that one up, too) and the FLH Electra Glide in 1965.

Maintaining the XL's separate images, H-D fitted an electric starter onto the XLH only in 1967.

This was done at some cost. The ground was prepared, so to speak, in 1965, when the XL line went from 6 volts to 12 because 1) the FL line needed 12 volts for the starter and 2) H-D engineering wanted all the twins to use the same generator.

The rest of the line remained as it was, except that because the XL frame didn't have room for one 12-volt

The hot-rod XLCH was still the fastest bike around in 1968. That would change the following year with the introduction of Honda's four-cylinder CB750.

battery, the Sportsters that year came with two 6-volt batteries. Oh, and all the models got levers with ball tips, not blades, in one of those safety moves that was so obvious when it was done that we can't imagine why it took so long.

The XLH gas tank was restyled, and capacity reduced to 3.7 gallons, because the shape was sleeker.

The 1966 model year was mostly XLCH as noted, except that the XLH also got the Tillotson carb and Hamcan air cleaner.

The Sportster's electric starter mounted behind the rear cylinder, above the gearbox, driving the clutch basket and spinning the engine via the primary chain. The drive was on the engine side of the clutch, so you could push the button with the tranny in gear if you had the clutch lever pulled in, meaning most riders learned to find neutral and then hit the button.

Working in house, we get some interesting comparisons, and some confusion.

The '67 XL engines were more alike than they looked. The CH retained the less bulky left side case half, and the magneto, fitted now with spark retard to help with cold starts. The XLCH retained the kicker, just in case. Both models had a big battery below the seat on the left, and the oil tank on the right. Because cold starts were easier, the full set of P camshafts was standard, and the XL engine was rated at 58 bhp, up from 55. Both models now came stock with an 18-inch rear wheel and 19-inch front, laced-up spokes.

Here's proof the factory took notes. Rick Conner's research shows that in model year 1966, the factory sold 3,900 XLCHs, compared with 900 in XLH trim.

For 1967, it was 2,000 for the XLH, 2,500 for the XLCH. And a major share of the electric-start buyers also got the shorty duals, peanut tank and even the smaller front fender. They liked the look of the sports bike, the easy starts of the formerly mild version.

Eventually Harley brought back the cast primary cover.

How so, formerly mild? Here's the confusion. *Cycle World* tested the all-sports XLCH with Linkert carb. It weighed 480 pounds at the curb, presumably topped up, and did the quarter-mile in 14.3 seconds.

That was in 1962, when the Superbike was just being invented. Just to keep the comparison fair, *Cycle* tested an XLCH in 1967, when the CH was kick and magneto. Power was rated at 60 bhp, curb weight was 461 pounds (presumably with empty tanks, and that was the lightest Sportster ever tested by disinterested parties). *Cycle* reported a quarter-mile ET of 14.1 seconds, and a top speed of 116 mph. The XLCH was fast, in so many words.

But early in 1968 *Cycle* tried the electric-start XLH, with points-and-coil ignition and the larger cases and all the mods required—and turned a 14.3 ET Curb weight now was 545 pounds. We do the math and the bottom line says 1) electric start adds 94 pounds and 2) the bulky '68 touring model is just as quick as the ferocious '62, putting out two or three more bhp while hauling nearly 100 pounds of extra weight.

Then in late 1968 *Cycle* tried the kick-only XLCH (really a 1969 model). Rated power was 58 bhp at 6,800 rpm, and the only visible change was a balance tube between the two head pipes just in front of the

mufflers. The factory said the pipe evened out the exhaust impulses and increased mid-range power, a claim rejected by all those who liked the looks of the staggered short duals.

There seems to have been something to it, though, because the 1969 XLCH clicked *Cycle*'s clocks at 13.65 seconds, a new record by a wide margin. And the curb weight—remember, this was all done by the same magazine under their own rules—was 470 pounds.

Sometimes, when you are in the testing business, all you can do is report the results. It doesn't seem possible that electric start added 85 pounds to the weight

of the XL. But if it did, how did the heavier bike get as quick or quicker with three or five extra bhp? And why was it 58 bhp sometimes and 60 bhp other times?

Because it just was, that's all. So the magazines simply reported what the scales and clocks told them.

The World Catches Up

Enthusiasts who were Harley-Davidson fans surely took some comfort from the tests cited here. They did show, minor questions aside, that the Sportster was easier to start and had lost none of its looks or performance as a result.

Solo seats were offered, and kept the weight down, but weren't as popular as the short two-up option.

*Bonneville on a Budget:
Amateur tuner Fritz Kott
swapped a dead car engine for
this XL engine, put it in a
leftover frame, modified the
engine at home . . . and set
four records at Bonneville, all
for beer and pizza money.*

But enthusiasts who were motorcycle fans had a different viewpoint.

The old rivals, the English makes, weren't standing still. While the domestic sporting mount had gone from a 45-cid side-valve twin to a 54-cid OHV twin, the sporting English machines had grown, too, from a 500-cc single to a choice of 650-cc Twins, with overhead valves, of course. (For the changes brought to racing by the changes on the street, see accompanying box.)

From another direction, literally, came a new and stronger and more permanent challenge.

Soichiro Honda was a gearhead's gearhead, a brilliant engineer and a man who literally changed the world. In later years, Mr. Honda said that while engineering played a major role, and his financial partner's skills were seldom appreciated, he reckoned the real secret was that he loved motorcycles. He'd think of a concept and say to himself, "I'd like a motorcycle like that. And if I'd like one, I bet the other bike nuts would, too."

Honda arrived with excellent little bikes that were attractive, reliable, and started with the push of a button. Then came little racers, and middleweights as good as the tiddlers. The 305s were followed by 350-cc twins, joined by 450 twins . . . and in 1969 Honda shocked the world with its 750 Four.

Well sure, fours had been with us since the Belgian FN of the early 'teens. But the Fours from Pierce and Henderson, later Ace and Indian, were either sedate gentlemanly tourers, or sturdy police packhorses.

The CB750 was different. The engine sat across the frame, so it was compact as well as powerful, and it offered power and smoothness and long engine life. Suffice it to say that the CB750 was, in real life, like all the other bikes were in the fulsome magazine reviews.

But wait, there was more. The other Japanese factories took different tacks to reach the American market. An East German designer had discovered the secret of two-stroke power, and an East German rider who'd helped in the race shop fled across the Iron Curtain with the secrets and signed with Suzuki.

Two-stroke quickly became the way to win races, worldwide first and later in the U.S.

The sporting two-strokes came to rule the streets, too. Suzuki twins and then Yamaha twins and most of all the Kawasaki triples—in 500-cc and 750-cc form— smoked (sorry, had to do it) the opposition. While it was true that Sportsters still won at the drags, it was equally true that while a *Cycle* tester, who had to be riding while holding his breath, could put an XLCH into the thirteens, as the racers say, a prepped-but-stock triple could dip into the twelves.

As a note combining the good news with the bad news, there are three reasons for buying a performance machine. The buyer is gonna go fast, the buyer believes he'll be going fast, or the buyer expects other people to think he'll be going fast and be impressed by his skill and daring. (We'll leave the percentages of the above for the cynics to estimate.)

The point here is that the sporting triples had more power than they had frame or suspension. *Cycle World* did a classic report on this fact, that the bike in question was the most overpowered and underchassied motorcycle ever made.

There was absolutely no way, the shaken *Cycle World* guy wrote, that any rider could hope to use all of

the performance the engine delivered.

He believed he was doing the world a favor, and perhaps he was, because the model under indictment sold out. Riding a bike that couldn't be tamed was a passport to the sort of approval a lot of buyers wanted.

And which they could no longer get from an XLCH, no matter how loud it was.

No one at The Motor Company has ever published the notes from the meetings, but in 1968 the kick lever was removed from the XLCH and all Sportsters got longer travel, and better control, in the front forks.

Top: *The peanut tank didn't hold much fuel, but it looked great.*

Above: *High pipes said this bike was meant to be ridden hard.*

THE SHORT, UNLIKELY HISTORY OF THE IRONHEAD XR-750

In 1968, after decades of good racing and partisan squabbles, the AMA's 750 side valve/500 overhead formula was abandoned.

With good reason. By the late 1960s, the sporting mounts of the early 1930s (i.e., 750-cc side-valve Harleys and Indians and 500-cc Triumph singles) had been eclipsed and the AMA (rightfully) wanted the national pro series to display performance beyond what the fans rode to the track.

The AMA also believed in making machines available to the public. All racers resent factory teams until they're asked to join one.

So the AMA competition board voted to have the 1969 dirt track races contested by 750s, produced in lots of 200, offered to the public but otherwise unlimited.

When the flag was waved, so to speak, Harley-Davidson was caught in neutral. The Motor Company was in financial trouble and was being acquired by a larger firm. It clearly hadn't bothered to plan for the inevitable day when the old KR would be pushed off stage.

Team manager Dick O'Brien and team engineer Peter Zylstra did the best they could. They didn't have the budget or time to produce a real, modern racing motorcycle. They did have the XLR, a winning TT bike in the right hands.

The 883-cc XLR engine was destroked, from 3.8 to 3.2 inches, which reduced the displacement to 747 cc, just inside the limit. They came up with a new set of camshafts, timed to spin the smaller engine faster, and they got to keep the magneto ignition, the quarter-speed oil pump and breather, and all the other specs already proven with the XLR, including— this is the bad part—the iron cylinders and heads.

The revised engine went into a revised frame, based on the late KRTT, with all steel tubing except for the lower rear engine mount castings. The top frame rails were extended back so the shocks (rear suspension was now allowed) and suspension components came from top makers Girling and Ceriani.

The project had all the earmarks of a jam session. The factory's first XR engine was built by Bill Werner, the team's top tuner, out of XL parts. The frames were farmed out to the Widman family, H-D dealers and racers in St. Louis, and the tank and seat were done by the Wixom brothers in California.

O'Brien told the AMA the machines would be ready for the 1969 season. He was known as a man of his word, so the AMA duly listed the XR-750, a designation completely in keeping with H-D practice, as an eligible competition model.

Now comes the part too good to be fiction. A privateer racer named Bob Butler knew what the Harley team planned to do, so he did it. Butler destroked his XLR and juggled the gears and when he showed up at the races early in 1969, he was allowed to race.

Then O'Brien, who was honest to a fault, told the AMA the XR-750 wouldn't be ready for the 1969 season, so the homologation was cancelled . . . but not before Bob Butler had raced a factory bike before the factory did.

The XR-750 was officially introduced at the opening event of the 1970 season in February at the Houston Astrodome. It was a big hit, arguably as attractive a motorcycle as has ever been made.

Then came disaster. The XLR had worked as a TT racer. That form of the sport calls for full power, full brakes, full power, and so forth. There had never been a question that aluminum would have been a better material. In fact, the FL Shovelhead was already on the scene and the factory made maybe a dozen sets of alloy heads for the XLR.

But cast iron's fatal flaw wasn't revealed until the 1970 Daytona 200, when all the new XRs melted and the team's honor was saved—well sort of—by the survival of a KRTT that finished in sixth place.

The iron block simply couldn't get rid of as much heat as the engine delivered, earning the engine the nickname "Waffle Iron" and costing defending AMA champ Mert Lawwill his title. (The story of that heartbreak is told in *On Any Sunday*. Don't miss it.)

O'Brien and crew draped the team XRs in oil coolers and came up with a series of three different two-carb conversions and wrenched competitive power out of the thing. But the flaw was permanent and the team lost the national title to Triumph rider Gene Romero in 1970 and BSA rider Gary Nixon in 1971.

The iron XR had one moment of glory, when road racer star Cal Rayborn and tuner Walt Faulk took Faulk's iron XRTT to England for the match race in 1972. Rayborn and Faulk made the trip on their own, because H-D execs expected public failure.

Instead, they got a legend. Rayborn won three of the six races and came in second three times, while Faulk spent every night rebuilding the bike, aided, he said later, by the damp and chilly English climate.

To this day, an English fan who sees an XR-750 will say, "Oh, like Rayborn's."

Back then, the factory made at least 200 XR-750s, that many were displayed for AMA inspectors, while there were also team bikes and so forth and an engine stamped #194 exists with cases numbered 225, hinting that there were spares.

The XR's troubles were quickly made public, and only an estimated 100 examples actually went out the factory's door. At the end of 1971, when the order book was blank, some of the leftovers were dismantled for parts and some were scrapped as a tax write-off.

The only bright spot has to be that O'Brien always said first, that the iron XR was always supposed to be a stopgap, the alternative to not going racing at all, and second, that what they learned with the iron engine was put to good use when AFM funded the alloy XR two years later.

In the longer run, the fact that the iron XRs blew up so early and often caused them to be parked in the back of scores of shops, with the result that when nostalgia was invented, somewhere between 35 and 50 survivors have been discovered, restored and in at least one case (the author's) is being raced in vintage events at this writing.

The first XR-750 was powered by a de-stroked XLR engine in a new (and better) frame, with a fiberglass version of the peanut tank, sort of, and fiberglass fender and seat base. Wheels are 19-in., as used in AMA pro racing. This example has been fitted with brakes for TT races.

Properly set up, the XLH made an excellent gentleman's touring bike. Jeff Hackett

The "H" meant a lot more to performance fans if it was preceded by a "C."

In 1969 the exhausts were joined by the infamous balance tube.

In 1970 the XLCH's magneto was replaced by the points-and-coil ignition the plain H had always had. In the pragmatic sense, this made kick-starting easier. In the intangible sense, because all the Sportsters now had the small headlight and the options of small or large fuel tank and thick or thin dual seat, the only difference between the two models was the electric leg.

This is a delicate subject, especially now, for reasons to be analyzed later. The Motor Company's founding families took The Company public, and when it was clear that wouldn't ensure its survival, the stockholders sold out to American Machine and

Foundry, a conglomerate at a time when being a conglomerate was trendy.

All we need to know about here is that AMF's execs had good intentions. Moreover, they were more comfortable investing in the plant than the product (and more in the product than the people).

Further, H-D had been doing some branching out on its own and had a fiberglass plant. Fiberglass was the carbon fiber of its day. It was thought to be the material of the future. So while GM was building Corvettes with fiberglass bodies, H-D was in the golf cart business. It also did some touring stuff and, like most other western motorcycle companies, experimented with ways to use the factory they already had.

The Harley-Davidson experiment, for the 1970 model year, was a boattail seat and fender option for the Sportster. It didn't look bad, in so many words, but it did look different. And the initial application was an

Even though the XLH was often outfitted as a touring bike, it was still a potent motorcycle. Jeff Hackett

A full set of instruments befitted a luxury touring bike. Jeff Hackett

answer to a question that the customers hadn't asked, i.e., the boattail option didn't sell.

What counts here is that Willy G. Davidson, grandson of one of the founders and at that time just coming into his own as a designer, took the boldest and most successful gamble of his career. In 1971 he borrowed the boattail seat and put it on an FL frame with an FL engine, an XL front end, and kick-start only. They called it the Super Glide (no hyphen, H-D only insists on the hyphen in its own name; the rest of the time they vary).

The Super Glide captured the public's attention, garnered a whole lot of ink, and in due course became the family of Super Glides that inspired all factory choppers, aka customs, and later cruisers. The civilized outlaw look became the style. In fact, it's still the style and the case can

be made that the Super Glide, secondhand fiberglass tail section notwithstanding, saved Harley-Davidson.

But that comes later, in another saga.

For here and then, the 1971 Sportsters traded the exterior ignition timer for points and condenser hidden behind a cap on the gearcase cover, and driven by the cams' gear trains.

The clutch, dry since the days of the Model K and KR, became wet. This was too bad, in that the dry clutch could use relatively light springs. But when the plates began running in oil, the spring was beefed up and so was the rider's clutch hand. This was good because the dry clutch soaked up gear lube no matter what the engineers did, but the 2004 racing XRs still use the dry clutch.

Previous page: *The windshield added an extra measure of comfort on a long ride.* Jeff Hackett

61

Top: *By 1968 the primary case had grown to accept the electric starter.* Jeff Hackett

Above: *Even though the foot shifter was on the left side of the Big Twin transmissions, Sportster mounted theirs on the right side, just like the British competition.* Jeff Hackett

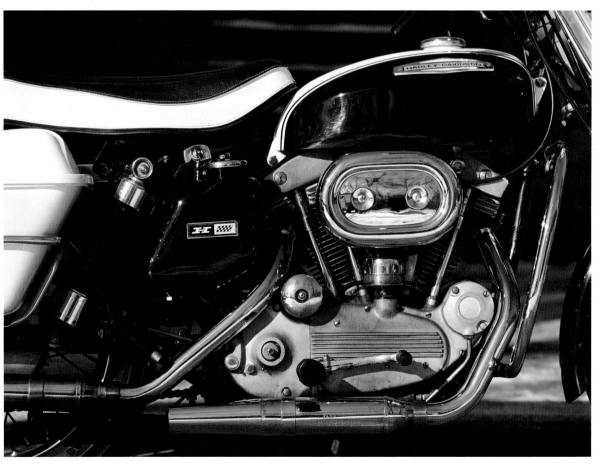

Sport-touring, circa 1968. From any angle, the XLH was a handsome bike. Jeff Hackett

Bottom line here was that none of this, the loss of ferocity and the displacement from the top of the performance heap, did any discernible damage.

There was a boom on, driven mostly by the terrifying two-strokes and the efficient little Hondas and the new hobby of off-road riding.

Even so, H-D got a good share of the enlarged pie, and the Sportsters were the best-selling models in the H-D line. According to Rick Conner 6,657 for the big twin, 4,700 for the Super Glide, and 10,775 for the XLs. And, yes, AFM had ramped up production, which led to quality problems but that, too, is a story for another place and time.

In terms of sales, service, and pride of ownership, the milder Sportsters were an unqualified success.

CHAPTER FIVE

THE
FIRST 1000s

The blacked-out ham-can air cleaner cleaned up the profile of the XLCR.

The alloy XR-750, introduced in 1972 but seen here in 1980 form, looked just like the earlier ironhead version, high dual exhausts excepted, with fiberglass tank and seat and even the stamped primary cover first seen on the XLCH.

Whoever first proclaimed "There's No Substitute for Cubic Inches" has been lost to history, but whoever it was, was right.

Or perhaps the secret was Yankee ingenuity. The story of the internal combustion engine has two sides to the displacement question; the aircraft side says decide what power you need and make the engine large enough to deliver that power without stress, and the tax side says when the government bases tax on size, make the engine small and tune for power.

U.S. companies (and governmental bodies) have favored the aircraft theory, while in Europe it's usually been tax-vs.-tune which, come to think of it, is the reason we got those previously mentioned racing rules of 750-cc side valve vs. 500-cc OHV.

In 1972, that meant that the Sportster family, which had gained weight, was required to meet new rules for noise (and a bit later, emissions). But it also needed to maintain at least some claim to sporting performance. So H-D engineers increased the XL engine's bore, from 3.00 inches to 3.18, raising the displacement from 883 cc/54 cid, to 1000/61.

The quibble here has long been that the 1,000-cc designation is shorthand for 997.l cc and the unrounded cid figure is 60.83, which is close enough to be fair.

As a history and marketing lesson, remember that the Model K shifted on the right, like the imports? In fact, the first Model E, the 1936 Knucklehead, was 61 cid and always known as the 61. This would have made a family link for the 61-cid XL, except that, again, the 1,000-cc XL was competing with imports and 1,000-cc compares favorably and easily with 750-cc.

Rated (or claimed) power was 61 bhp, a new high and useful because it was power from torque; i.e., pulling and climbing power.

(As another odd side note: The increased bore brought some shifting of components. While it can be done, it's not worth swapping later iron-top barrels and heads for the earlier version. It's one example of a time when the factory's policy of allowing updates wasn't practical.)

This was an era of gradual and sudden-but-shocking change.

How so?

Very little fuss was made at the time, but just as the difference between the plain H and the CH faded away, so did the choice of solo or dual seat. The single seat went out of fashion in the mid to late '60s, and by 1972 it was replaced by a semi-custom seat, thinner and firmer and molded to the fender in a style seen on early home-built choppers.

The alloy XR had new cases, space-age alloy cylinders and heads, dual carbs, cranks out more than 100 bhp and has been winning races and titles for 30-plus years.

Harley Team manager Dick O'Brien, who led the squad and fought the political battles from 1957 until he retired in 1983, always defended the iron XR-750 because the work done on that ill-starred machine resulted in the alloy XR-750, the dirt track version of which has become the winningest racing motorcycle in history.

This is the flip side (the down side) of that story.

When the AMA revised the national championship series in 1954, the underlining belief was that a true champion had to be an all-arounder. The professional, nationwide series was contested on short tracks, half-miles, miles, and TT, all with dirt surfaces, and on road courses. When the concept was created, a rider could use one machine, refitted with shocks or brakes, a different tank or whatever, for all five types of races.

This was later changed, but in the time frame here, the road race portions of the series were run with 750-cc engines, as offered for public sale, produced in quantities of at least 200. There was plenty of scope for later modification, but that's the outline.

The iron XR appeared in 1970, blew up early and often, cost H-D the national title, and didn't sell.

In 1972 Harley-Davidson announced the new XR-750. It had new cylinders and heads made with space-age alloy, a larger bore and shorter stroke, two carburetors, more improvements than can be listed here, and as much power its first day as the iron version had on its last.

The alloy XR shared only the primary drive, clutch, and ignition with the iron XR and almost no parts with the XL models. But H-D kept the XL profile and the designation, presumably for marketing reasons, although the XRs have always been kept as quiet as the rules allow.

Road racing was O'Brien's favorite part of the series and the best place to get the import buyer's attention. So the team's road race bikes got some special treatment.

They used wraparound versions of the XR frame, the excellent fairings developed for the late KRTTs, and big tanks. The first year saw lightweight rear disc brakes and generous four-shoe drum brakes in front. As soon as they could, the Harleys switched to Honda discs, listed in the parts book with Honda's help (no kidding).

The XRTT, so called because of the old rules for brakes and suspension, was a competitive mount. Cal Rayborn won two of the 1972 season's seven road races and Mark Brelsford won the AMA title.

But the era was about to close. The 1972 Daytona 200 went to Don Emde on a 350 Yamaha two-stroke twin. While attrition helped, none of the old guard ever expected such a role reversal.

Then, things got worse. When the old line clubs drew up the rules, they knew from experience that factories had limits.

What they hadn't predicted is that Yamaha meant to win, and cost was no object. Yamaha was a conglomerate, just as Harley-Davidson was part of AMF. But where AMF treated its divisions as a source of income, Yamaha used its sum to support its parts, which is to say first they doubled the twin into the TZ700, an inline two-stroke four with more power than any four-stroke 750 ever dreamed of. Then they made 200 units, shipped them to the U.S. for homologation . . . and they changed racing forever. The American, English, Italian, and German makes would be out of contention in road racing for the next generation. The next Daytona win by a four-stroke—or a non-Yamaha—wouldn't come until 1985.

The XRTT thus became history, through no fault or flaw of its own. The project must have taken a good chunk of the racing department's modest budget. Now it was all for naught. The plan had been to build ten examples for the team and 40 more to be sold to selected privateers. But in an unhappy and ill-fated repeat of the first XR debacle, the privateers bought elsewhere and the later examples of the XRTT frame were scrapped or shuffled out of the shop's back door to select O'Brien beneficiaries. The engines and drivetrain parts could be and were fitted to the XR-750 dirt bikes (more on that later).

Ironically, the happy ending is the soaring popularity of vintage racing, coupled with the rule that allows updates for old engines. Thanks to Harley's policy of gradual change, a 1972 XRTT can be legally improved to the extent that some vintage clubs impose restrictor plates because the Harleys otherwise lap the field.

Oh, those Yamahas! Having proved the point, Yamaha shipped all but a handful back home, never to be seen again.

Next page: *The legendary Calvin Rayborn, at speed and in control, on his way to 4th place in the Imola (Italy) 200, 1973. The XRTT was a match for the other production fourstrokes but not for the Yamaha TZ700. This is the full XRTT, with Wixom Bros fairing and seat and with a scavenge tank for the oil system visible below the fairing's two sides.* Jim Greening photo

The 1977 XLCR attempted to capture the excitement of the XR750, but it was basically a gussied up version of the XLH.

There was a lot going on between the lines, so to speak. During the early and mid '70s, H-D designers also got as far as a mockup, perhaps even a prototype, of an overhead cam 750-cc twin. Yes, no kidding. Photos (no longer available due to current Motor Company policy) show a semi-chopper seat, a gas tank direct from the XR-750 and an OHC V-twin, with a 750-cc label.

The folks at H-D knew what was going on outside the walls. But they had budget constraints and production problems, and just as they stuck with cast iron because alloy could have been trouble, so did the overhead cam middleweight never get through the door.

Instead, in 1973 the Sportster got a replacement frame.

Careful here. The frame wasn't new, in that it still had the iron junctions, the shocks mounted forward on the swing arm, and had separate ball bearings cupped in the steering head.

But the rear casting did away with the posts for the suspended solo seat now out of fashion (and production). And the steering head was pulled back one degree, from 30 to 29 degrees, quickening the steering and shortening the nominal wheelbase by a fraction . . . and allowing the use of Kayaba front forks.

Yes. Imported from Japan. The new forks were of course top quality, no question there. And the official policy has always been, and still is, that when the manufacturer can't find a domestic supplier, the only choice is to import. Hard to argue, albeit we seldom know how hard the factory looked before accepting the low bid.

In that same model year, and much more visibly, the Sportster got a disc front brake. This was a clear improvement, the only puzzle being why the motorcycle makers waited for several years after the car guys had proved the disc better in every way.

And, for the genuine shocker, one the new enthusiast will have trouble believing, the Sportster, indeed all the Harley twins, got . . . a throttle return spring.

Black paint, gold trim and the classic peanut tank made the later iron Sportsters look more sporting than they actually were. And the feds moved the shift from the right to the left, and the brake pedal from the left to the right.

Wow, eh? Right, all these years Harleys came with the lowest-possible-tech cruise control. You turned the grip to how fast you wanted to go, and it stayed there until you rolled on or off. None of the riders who began this way ever found it to be that tough a deal, in a way like the racers who rode when brakes were banned, while those who have never done it find it hard to believe.

There must have been several factors here. The federal government was becoming involved, as we'll see shortly, and H-D was making an effort to attract riders who hadn't ridden Harleys before. And there was now a Bendix carburetor, with a butterfly throttle that may have worked best with a spring.

The federal government officially got into the act in 1975.

The need for legal force can be debated, in that when the pioneer car builders realized early in the twentieth century that their customers would be happier if all cars had the same basic controls, they agreed on the clutch-brake-throttle pedal sequence, and on the H-pattern gearshift. (OK, Henry Ford dragged his feet, but the principle applies.)

By the mid 1970s, virtually all motorcycles had foot shift and hand clutch, but the shifter sequence and location varied. A lot. Some shifted up, some down, some were on the right, others on the left, with neutral occasionally at the bottom or even at the top.

The differences were as much defended as the solution was debated. But in 1975 that all changed when the federal government mandated that the gearshift lever be on the left, with first gear down, all others up, and neutral between first and second.

Big Harleys and all Hondas were already configured this way, so the burden fell heaviest on the English, who were about to go out of business anyway. And, of course, the Sportster, which had the gear lever on the right to lure import riders (remember?).

The 1975 solution, so to speak, was a trade. A swap. Sportsters were fitted with linkages that moved the gearshift to the left and brake pedal to the right. It wasn't neat but it wasn't noticed much, either. And that postponed some expensive revision.

The 1976 Sportsters were carryovers, as they say in the trade, with the emphasis on paint. In 1976, USA's

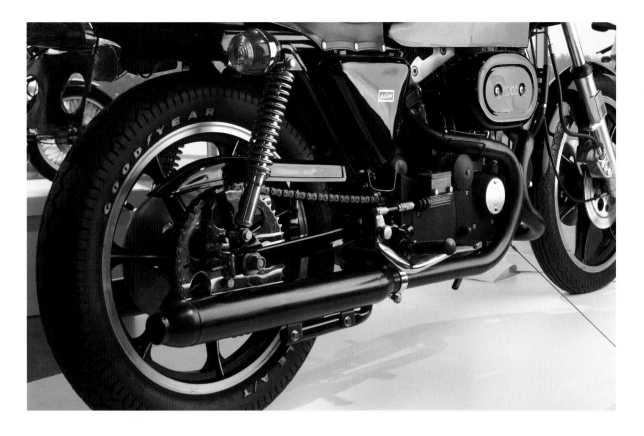

The XLCR's Siamesed pipes were unique and may even have added some mid-range power.

By 1978 only the peanut tank harkened back to the Sportster's performance roots.

bicentennial, H-D celebrated by offering paint schemes called Liberty Editions done up in red, white, and blue.

The Sportster had more parts than it carried ten years earlier. The kick starter was history, the exhaust note subdued, and the kick-butt championship had gone elsewhere.

Even so, *Cycle World* and *Cycle* both tested Sportsters during this time period. Both weighed their machines at close to 500 pounds, and both returned quarter-miles in the high thirteens. *Cycle*'s test was quicker because they ran the 49-state model, while *Cycle World*'s example came with a California muffler, which was more restrictive.

These were not slow motorcycles. In fact, they were easily the quickest Harleys, as always.

Furthermore, the 1975 Sportsters outsold the newly-electric-legged Super Glide by two to one, with the FLH way behind both, so the public was still voting for the model.

CHAPTER SIX

STYLE
AND STEEL

The 1978 (75th) Anniversary XLH borrowed lots of cruiser or chopper touches, as sales figures showed the public was headed in that direction.

The XLCR used expanded versions of the XR-750's tank and seat, with a frame that extended back to above the rear axle, with a siamesed dual exhaust and with shades and textures of black everywhere you looked.

There can't be many people who've done a better job playing the cards life dealt them than Willie G. Davidson.

Grandson of one of The Motor Company's founding fathers, Willie G. was raised in a town where his name was on the factory, went away to college (to study design), worked where he had no family for a couple of years and then joined the company where Granddad was a founder and Dad was president.

It's easy to imagine how easily he could have done little, or reached for more than he could grasp. Instead, Willie G. proved to have an excellent eye for style, a feel for what the public will like before the public knows, and the ability to keep his feet on the ground.

His first major project as head of the design department was the Super Glide, the mix of F-series drivetrain and frame with X-series front end, plus a look that was street tough. It's been argued that the FX Super Glide set the tone for H-D sales success, inspired all those metric cruisers and kept The Motor Company in business.

The Café Racer

And sometimes, as the saying goes, the bear eats you. In the 1960s, while American shade tree stylists were creating the chopper with the elements of the big twin TT racers from the 1940s and '50s, in Europe the same mindset was building street racers mimicking road race machines; rear-set footpegs, dropped handlebars, tiny fairings, huge brakes, and pipes as loud as the builder could get away with. The fashion was racing from hangout to hangout. And because the crowd gathered at coffee shops, some clever chap called these modified bikes Café Racers.

They were all the fashion in Europe, and they had a small following in the U.S. (smaller than some folks thought, as we'll note shortly).

Willie G.'s name was still on the factory, but the families no longer owned the firm, so he had to rely on work and skill (from both himself and his partners).

AMF's policy was to make as many bricks with as little straw as possible, as in making new models with existing parts, witness the Super Glide. So Davidson, Jim Haubert, and Bob Moderow launched a major project using as many Sportster components as they could, loosely inspired by the café racer fad and named—as the reader will have already guessed—the XLCR (no prizes for what the letters stood for).

The biggest change was the frame. The Sportster frame mounted the shock absorbers below the seat at the top, midway between the hub and the pivot at the swingarm. When the design appeared in 1952 on the K

The front of the exhaust snaked around and in front of the frame and back to a muffler well to the rear. The plastic panel below the front of the seat covers the battery and electrical gear.

In general, this update of frame and suspension was patterned on the XR-750 frame, as the press release reported, although there were actually no shared parts.

Next came the exhaust system, done in matte black and with both head pipes merged below the carb and then separated. The forward pipe swept back to the left and then to a muffler on the left, true duals and responsible—the factory claimed—for a boost to 68 bhp from the otherwise shared XL-1,000 engine.

The fiberglass seat and rear fender sort of resembled the XR-750's seat, while the seat pad itself used snaps, just like the XR's. The flaw here was that to keep that license plate and taillight away from the rear tire, the fender had to jut clumsily back, where the XR's flowed gracefully.

The gas tank also was inspired by the XR, except it was bigger, at 4.0 gallons, than either the XR or the XL's peanut tank. In front was a small fairing, a bikini fairing as we said then, because it didn't cover much. At speed, though, the fairing would keep some air pressure off the rider's chest.

The CR got cast wheels, more a modern than a café racer touch, and disc brakes front and rear. And at the same time the XL cases were reworked to allow the shift lever to emerge from the left side of the gearbox, and the rear brake got a master cylinder, so there were no more crossings over.

Willie G. and staff did the décor in shades of black, as in matte for the pipes, wrinkle for the covers, paint for the rest, with a bronzed bar-and-shield for the tank badges.

The pegs and controls were rear-set, the handlebars were narrowed and the front fender was small and made of fiberglass, which did meet the café rules.

Because this was supposed to perform, the gearing was changed, with one tooth taken off the engine sprocket. The CL turned more revs at any road speed than the stock CH, which was supposed to be an aid to acceleration. Which it did, to the tune of an E.T. of 13.08 seconds.

Top: *Bikini fairing provides some wind protection if the rider crouches, a posture dictated by the low drag-style handlebars.* Above: *The XLCR's tail section is longer and less graceful than the XR-750's, but the street version had to have some place for lights and plate.*

Model, it made sense. By 1972 or 1975, when the idea for the CR was hatched or the design begun, the XL's frame was woefully out of date.

So the junction became history. Aft of the backbone the CR had two smaller rails, extended back to above the rear hub, and triangulated with tubes to the rear engine mount. The shocks mounted directly above the hub. There was less flex, improved control, and room to neatly mount the oil tank and battery that extruded, so to speak, with the original XL design.

Speedometer and tachometer were standard equipment for the anniversary model, along with the minimum number of warning lights.

(Historical note: Harley's press guy conned the test rider into revealing the test times before publication, which was against *Cycle World*'s rules. He then called *CW*'s editor and threatened legal action if the figures were published. When the editor told him CBS, the magazine's owner at the time, kept a cage full of attorneys just waiting for such action, the PR guy settled for hiring his own rider. They tested at dawn when it's cool and the air more dense, and used those times, in the high 12s, in the Café Racer's ads.)

It's therefore highly ironic that the Café Racer was a commercial failure. The first batch sat in dealer showrooms until the prices went down. The next year they revised so there was space for a passenger, and after that the model left the catalog.

Why the flop? Magazine comments of the day show the CR did perform well, easily on par with the other sporting twins if not the powerhouse fours from Japan's Big Four.

The CR did have a better frame, could cruise for more miles, had better brakes and extra power and the crouch plus fairing made it heaps more comfortable on the highway than the laidback slump of the cruiser, a fad just then hatched.

But Conner's figures show nearly 17,000 of the CH and H designation, virtually identical except for details like handlebars, out the door in 1977, against 1,923 XLCRs. In 1978, production slumped to 1,201.

Now the irony flips over. In the long and practical run the CR's frame was an improvement, likewise the cast wheels which can use tubeless, make that modern, tires. The work wasn't wasted.

The other factor that worked in its favor is the collector mentality, which likes to put itself above the crowd. So when the crowd turns something down, as happened to the CR, the collectors take interest and start bidding.

And that's what's happened to the XLCR. The common XL from the 1970s is bought and sold as a

Right: *The anniversary model was mostly cosmetic emphasis, for instance the antique type face used on the tank decals. The 2-into-1 exhaust system was a carryover.* Far right: *Crowded, eh? The addition of the electric starter and the need for a bigger battery have made the center of the '78 XLH a busy place.*

Major moves came with the 1979 XL; the frame was extended to the rear, as first seen with the XR-750 and the XLCR. Moving the shocks back allowed the oil tank and battery to be tucked away behind tidy panels. Cast wheels were an option. This was the first year for the 16-in. rear wheel. Cycle magazine photo.

motorcycle, while for cafe racers there's an owners' club and websites and a brisk trade in decals and original parts and exhaust systems and the like, for what Willie G. must have considered a bubble on his paint.

The XLT

A more modest and parallel project, still working to get extra models with minimum expense, came along at the same time. (There's a hedge here because some sources list this as a 1977 model that was sold in 1976, some say 1977 on both counts.)

This also begins with style. Early in the 1960s H-D bought Aermacchi, an Italian bike maker that had fallen

on hard times (just as Harley could no longer afford to make lightweight models in the U.S.). Aermacchi had an excellent line of four-stroke singles, imported here and sold as the Sprint.

The sporting Sprint had a 3.5-gallon fuel tank that was as shapely a design as ever seen on a motorcycle. True Italian styling and it looked so good on the Sprint that in 1974 the teardrop tank replaced the dual F-model tanks on the Super Glide.

For model year 1977, the XL line was expanded. With the XLT, the T stood for Touring and the addition had the large and lovely tank, a thicker and much more comfortable seat, higher handlebars, a windshield, an

extra tooth on the countershaft sprocket to drop engine revs on the highway, and luggage bags from the FLH.

This was a bet on the other side of the coin, you could say, a hope that just as some buyers wanted extra sport and, um, European notions, there were others who'd like a lighter and more compact version of the King of the Highway FLH.

Again, there were benefits to the lowered gearing, the extended range, and the weather protection and comfort and luggage capacity.

And again, the public shrugged. In 1977 XLT total sales were 1,099, less even than the XLCR.

All this fuss brought some genuine improvement. Cast wheels, 18-inch rear, 19-inch front, as seen first on the CR, became an option for the full line in 1978.

Model year 1979 brought major upgrades, as the extended frame became standard. There was some juggling needed here, with the new locations for the battery and oil tank moving the rear brake master cylinder and linkage. The kick-starter disappeared, and with it the XLCH model name. Not a big thing, as for the previous five years the kick lever and small tank option had been all the CH really was.

Marketing then got into the act. The XLCR and XLT were gone from the catalog, while the Super Glide

Federal noise rules mandated the larger and bulgy air cleaner. The siamesed exhaust system was carried over from the XLCR. Cycle magazine photo.

had become a model line with a version called the Low Rider. This was another click of the chopper dial, as in dropped rear, raised front, and so forth.

Someone in the sales and planning department noticed this. If the Sportster buyers don't want European fads, and they don't want miniature highway haulers, could they be looking for the chopper image?

Credit here to AMF, in that the execs were willing to take chances. They introduced the XLS, which was a puzzling choice because it wasn't Sport. Instead, there was a contest for a name and the winner was Roadster; clearly they couldn't call it the XLR, or the XLC, could they? Nor were we ever told what the other entries in the name contest were.

The S must stand for Style. The Roadster introduced a 16-inch rear wheel, adding visual muscle, and had extended forks, two inches longer than the XLCH used. The gas tank was the shapely teardrop carried over from the XLT, short handlebars were mounted on dog-bone risers, as was done by the backyard guys and shops of the day.

The seat was lower while the suspension was raised. The bars were flatter but the mounts were higher, which means the actual ergonomics were the same but the look was different.

Most subtle was the reworking of the rear frame and the siting of the components. One of the unwritten nuggets of wisdom within The Motor Company is that the true Harley-Davidson buyer cannot stand to see the frame rails because real Harleys, the ones his granddad rode, didn't have frame rails below or aft of the seat.

The 1980 Sportsters thus juggled the parts and concealed the frame rails.

The verdict? Well first, this means that to this day the catalogs for exhaust systems and such caution that the gear for pre- or post-79 won't fit the bikes made that model year.

Next, the Roadster name didn't catch on, but the model did fairly well, keeping the differences and

the name until the ironhead XLs went out of production. So the sales and styling guys won some return on AMF's bet.

The Hugger

Folklore notwithstanding, women did not just last year fling away their corsets and discover motorcycles.

Women have always ridden motorcycles, albeit they replaced skirts and corsets and bonnets with jodhpurs and caps and then jeans and helmets.

However, about the time regular guys were willing to be seen on Harleys, it became something of, well, a fad, for women to ride solo.

In model year 1980, without ever actually saying so, Harley-Davidson made riding easier for the gentler gender.

The model was—and still is—Hugger. It was an option. The Hugger had shorter shock absorbers and fork legs, and a thinner seat, all of which lowered the machine.

Women in general are shorter and lighter than men, and have less strength, especially in the upper body. The lowered Sportster, with an official seat height of 26 inches that first year, and with minor changes since, was easier to throw a leg over, heave off the sidestand, balance in slow going and at rest, with feet planted on the ground. There are several states that require the rider to be able to put both feet down, an even better incentive.

Sure, there were some drawbacks. The ride height and seat thickness hadn't been picked without reason. The lower ride height meant stiffer springs and shocks to handle the bumps and potholes. The thinner seat meant more shocks got through to the rider.

It didn't matter. There were enough women—and surely some guys who were either short or liked the looks of the lowered XLH—to keep the model in production ever since.

But just as the car people have learned, you can sell a young man's car to an old man, and a man's car to a

woman, but neither works in reverse. So the Hugger has never been advertised as a woman's motorcycle.

Real Steel

Back with traditional Motor Company practice, the Sportster had benefited from the larger engine, the electric start, the new carburetor and suspension, and the revisions and additions to the model lineup.

It was time for another leap.

It came for model year 1982, with a new frame.

The dimensions weren't much changed and the extended rear portions were the same, but the cast-iron steering head was replaced with steel, welded not brazed (as 007 would say).

The new frame was lighter and stronger and stiffer. This wasn't a mixed bag. Racing designers learned years ago that there is an optimum stiffness for a frame in terms of torsion, and that you need the stiffness so the suspension has something against which to brace itself.

It's also a safe bet that manufacturing techniques had evolved and it was now more practical to weld all the steel parts together than it was to weld some of the tubes and braze the iron junctions to them.

In any case, the '82 model Sportsters got the best frame the XL family had ever had.

With that, now that the suspension had something to work against, the shock absorbers and front forks were upgraded at the same time. Oh, and the suspension components were now imported from Japan. H-D has always said no domestic suppliers will bother with the low numbers involved with motorcycles, and that may be so, but it does put a useful damper on excessive flag waving.

The AMF Question

Notetakers will recall that late in the 1960s Harley-Davidson had become a publicly traded company, with the founding families still holding much of the stock. The company was also in financial trouble and was the subject of takeover attempts, one hostile and one friendly.

The friendly buyer was American Machine and Foundry, better known as AMF. The timing was terrible, because in the early 1970s the world's governments imposed rules and controls on the world's vehicle makers. Engineers were diverted to emissions and safety projects and quality control paid the price. This happened to other motorcycle makers, and to the car companies. Just ask anyone about a 1970 Ferrari, a 1972 Plymouth, or even (cover your ears if strong language offends) an English Rover.

Point here comes in two parts: One, AMF has been criticized for things not entirely their fault and two, after 10 years of hard work and investment, AMF decided to sell H-D. The Motor Company's top execs and relatives of the founders borrowed all they could and pledged all they had and bought Harley-Davidson back.

They, the new owners that is, had the plant and the plans. They had a running start on the product, and what they needed was basic; money and time.

In the shortest term, and in Sportster terms, they kept the old reliable 1, 000-cc, iron-top XL engine, with the new and improved frame and suspension. They dropped labels like XLCH and relied on quick tricks like

raised buckhorn handlebars, sissy bars and—because 1982 was the Sportster's 25th anniversary—paint schemes to celebrate.

Not that this was a bad thing. *Cycle World* tested an '82 XLH and came away impressed. The gearing had been raised to reduce buzz, but the bike still turned the quarter mile in 14.26 seconds, enough to beat a Corvette or Porsche of the day, even though the emissions rules had required the compression ratio to be reduced from 9:1 to 8:1, thanks to thicker head gaskets. That plus quieter exhaust pipes and a new air cleaner reduced delivered power to an estimated 50 bhp.

It was, as Rolls-Royce used to say, enough to do the job.

High bars, stepped seat, dual disc brakes in front, lots of black paint, the 1982 XLH looks like the previous model, except that the exhaust pipes are once again staggered duals, and the new frame is stronger and lighter.

CHAPTER SEVEN

A BOLD MOVE… AND A BARGAIN: 1983-1985

The XR1000 came out at a time when Harley-Davidson was in its darkest hours. Jeff Hackett

Perhaps the major reason AMF is defended by those who can look beyond the political view of history is that the conglomerate make investments in the product as well as the plant.

At the same time, to be fair to the critics, the results of this policy sometimes took a long time to surface. And even the new owners, heroes though they were, didn't always know what to do with what they had.

The XR1000 was an important motorcycle for Harley-Davidson in 1983.

The XR-1000

We'll open this part of the saga with a bold move . . . that failed.

Professional racing in the U.S., first in all and later some of its forms, has relied on Harley-Davidson machines and motivation for, oh, call it 75 years, ever since 750-cc Harley twins became the median racing motorcycle.

Late in the 1960s, the AMA rules were changed to allow production 750-cc machines (as noted earlier). And while some vocal types clamored about a café racer they didn't later buy, there were other racing fans who wanted an XR-750 for the street.

There were some so keen they actually did the project themselves, or hired racing tuners to do it during the off season. And it made sense (well, sort of) because those early XR-750s used basic XL parameters. You could install a Sportster kick-start, generator, and magneto, even a drum front brake or racing discs front and back. Put tiny mufflers on the drag-style pipes, find a state inspector who shared your enthusiasm and, presto, you're riding to work on a motorcycle previously seen racing TT at Ascot.

A handful of true believers did it. Many more fans thought about it—or talked about it—to the extent that late in the 1970s guys in the racing and engineering departments on Juneau Avenue made few prototypes of

an XR-750 that were modified to meet the new federal regulations just then coming into force.

They decided, not happily, that while one builder could fit a racing motorcycle with enough equipment to tiptoe past state regulations, an international maker couldn't do the same job meeting all the new rules

The full set of gauges hinted at the performance potential of the XR1000.

The exhaust pipes on the left side of the bike let fans know that something really different was going on here.
Jeff Hackett

Dual carbs and aluminum heads were based on those used on the XR750 racer.

with higher limits. Such a model would have had maybe 30-35 bhp and weigh more than 400 pounds. Not what the street XR buyer had in mind.

The notion didn't go away. Instead, racing department boss Dick O'Brien was instructed to work with his guys and the engineers and compliance department to see what sort of performance model could be built to meet the limits and mimic the race bikes.

"Challenge" doesn't begin to define such a project.

What no one in The Motor Company's management ranks seemed to realize is the old folk wisdom that "Everything Is Harder Than It Looks."

The basic idea was to bolt the XR-750's two-carb alloy heads to the XL-1000's iron cylinders and lower end, cases, gearbox, and so forth.

It didn't work that way. The plan called for the stock, all-steel XL frame, which as mentioned was an excellent design. But it was bigger and heavier than the chrome-moly steel frame used for the 750 racer. And the alloy heads and XL barrels were too tall for the XL frame . . . and by the time the six-month deadline arrived, they knew they needed new cases, and cylinders, and modified heads, and shorter connecting rods, and special . . . well, you get the idea.

Further, because the racing shop was just a couple of guys and the production lines weren't used to precise machine work, the factory subcontracted the heads to tuner Jerry Branch, who had the skill but not a large workforce. He could agree only to a contract for 4,500 heads, as in 2,250 engines, per year.

As it happened, limited production wasn't the problem.

Instead—and how this came about is still worth debating—the marketing team had completely missed the point.

Hold that thought.

The other H-D news for model year '83 was, as will be noted next, the XLX, a basic price-buster, stripped of all extras.

As has been proven since the days of modified chariots, when you're selling something special it must look special. Closer to home, the 1971 Super Glide looked new and different from blocks away, looked more different than it actually was, and it sold so well the model became a family of models. Ford and Chevrolet made Thunderbird and Corvette engines available in sedans, while in fact the sports cars were using sedan engines.

Point made? OK, so when H-D had done all the engineering and had this limited-edition, high-performance engine, they jammed it into a standard frame, and dressed it like an XLX, tiny solo seat and peanut tank.

And they painted it gray. Yes, gray. The factory team's racing colors had been black and orange with white since the Daytona-winning team of 1968.

This isn't to say the XR-1000 wasn't good in ways that should matter.

Cycle World introduced the model on the cover of the March 1983 issue. The *CW* crew was impressed,

As attractive as the bike was, the package really didn't work all that well. Jeff Hackett

first because the XR-1000 was quick, a street-stock Harley record of 12.88 seconds for the quarter-mile. And because the new frame and centered mass made it an excellent sports bike, it was at home on challenging roads and equal to the challenge from the imports.

The testers detailed how the project had been carried out and the changes made and gave high marks for the work that had been done.

At the same time, as an honest magazine, they noted some quirks.

One, the high, dual exhausts down the left side got hot and stayed hot, which might not matter during the 25 minutes a pro rider sits during a mile national, but reduced the fun during an afternoon in the skimpy saddle.

Mounting the XR750-style top end on an XL-based Streetbike was an ambitious idea that suffered from a hasty execution.

Next page top: *The XL883 appeared before Harley had universally switched to belt final drive.*

Next page bottom: *Even with a twin-disc front brake, stopping power was marginal by contemporary standards. Braking wouldn't be up to modern standards until the 21st century.*

Two, putting the engine where it had to be and the exhaust where it had to be, shifted the longitudinal center of gravity. "The XR-1000 has to list a few degrees to the right in order to stay balanced," the reviewers said. "This means when it's ridden straight down the road, the rider needs to add a slight amount of steering to the left to keep the bike upright."

And while the engine produced more power than the plain XLH, it used more fuel. The standard *CW* mileage test then was two 50-mile loops followed by a careful fill-up. In this test, though, the bike went onto reserve before the second loop could be completed and the rider dared not risk getting back to the shop. So the mpg, 46 to be exact, was recorded after one loop.

Quoting the test again, "All this makes the XR-1000 not your perfect bike for a casual trip to the corner market—commitment is called for," the review said.

And then comes the question of price. Robert Evans, a New Jersey police officer who knows more about the XR-1000 than anyone else on the planet, says he was told that the suggested retail price for the XR-1000 was first supposed to be $5,000, or $1,000 more than the XLX, which seemed reasonable. Next time the planners met it was $6,000. And when the model was announced, it was $7,000 and the outsiders said to themselves "too much."

Further, the XR came with two front disc brakes. This was good, but required a hefty squeeze to get results. The test bike weighed 500 pounds, with half a tank of fuel.

An iron XR-750 equipped with dual discs, mufflers, kick-start, tiny battery, and lights weighs 365 pounds. With 2.25 gallons of gas. A race-ready alloy XR-750 goes to the starting line a bit over 300 pounds, with 100 bhp, by the way.

The XR-1000 engine was rated at 70 bhp at a time when the standard XLH delivered 50 bhp.

So the alloy heads, twin carburetors, and dual exhaust did give more power and performance.

Even though the XR1000 had mechanical issues, it made money for the Motor Company.

But check the notes. The XLH had a lower compression ratio and used a mild set of camshafts that were shared with the XR-1000. A canny buyer could take the bargain XLX, swap for the earlier camshafts, raise the compression ratio, fit a bigger carb, free-flowing air cleaner and exhaust pipes and get that 70 bhp with money left over for, oh, orange and black paint and a dual seat. Why impress the women if you can't take 'em home?

The XLX

Keep the Evans quote in mind. Newly independent Harley-Davidson needed sales and they had some history to overcome (never mind that AMF wasn't the villain H-D literature would later claim it was).

Sales philosophy (if there is such a thing) will surely say that price may sometimes be an object, while price is always an excuse, a reason to buy or not to buy.

The slim Sportster profile made an ideal platform for a performance bike.

WINNING THE WHOLE
NEW BALL GAME

None of us can really be sure we understand another person's true agenda. So it's merely guesswork to wonder what H-D's racing director had in mind when he agreed to head the XR-1000 project.

The guesswork begins with Dick O'Brien's known enthusiasm for racing—road racing in particular—and his frustration when in the 1970s the multi-cylinder two-strokes took command of the paved courses. They eclipsed the four-stroke twins, from Triumph, BSA, Norton, BMW, Ducati, and Moto Guzzi, as well as from Harley-Davidson.

But then, 10 years after the XRTT—loosely but legally based on the XL engine, remember—was withdrawn from road race competition, the AMA responded to the loss of factory and fan support with a new class called Battle of the Twins, open to—yes!—four-stroke twins powered by 1000-cc engines based at least on production road machines.

So there was O'Brien, asked to ramrod the road-going XR-1000 late in 1982, as the class was being organized. Better still, the rules simply said the engine had to be sort of like the production engine. For instance, it had to retain the stock bore and stroke and the number of carburetors—while every other detail was pretty much open.

This was at a time when no one on the payroll could be sure there would be a check that week. There was no budget for racing.

Better, there was talent and drive and a workshop from which nothing had ever been thrown away.

Four-time national champion Carroll Resweber dug out the remains of the XRTT frame crashed at Daytona in 1973 by then champ Mark Brelsford. Resweber knew the best road racer ever on the Harley team was the late Cal Rayborn, and he knew the specs and dimensions Rayborn preferred. So Resweber rebuilt the frame as a Rayborn replica, except for modern items like stronger forks, better disc brakes, and 18- (later 16-) inch wheels.

The (nominal) XR-1000 engine used XR-750 cases and internals,

topped by very special cylinder heads O'Brien had created years earlier and tucked under the bench for just such an opportunity.

Tank, seat and fairing were the old XRTT parts because they worked then and worked still. The bike got modern ignition, electronic not magneto, and better carburetors and an oil tank that sat below the cases for a lower center of gravity, and a long, thin shape to put more surface in the airstream.

O'Brien had a flair for drama and named the machine "Lucifer's Hammer" which he said came from Celtic mythology. Never mind that no such myth has ever been found in the folklore collections, it made for good headlines.

Better headlines were made at Daytona Beach in 1983.

O'Brien assigned Jay Springsteen, a three-time AMA number one despite riding only dirt when the rival Yamaha team had dirt and pavement bikes, to contest the BOT feature.

In 2004, Louis Netz is head of styling at The Motor Company. But in 1983 he was second in command to Willie G.

Netz was seated at the infield U-turn of Daytona Speedway's road course when Springsteen entered the turn, followed by Team Ducati's Jim Adamo, the reigning BOT champion.

Adamo showed Springsteen a wheel, as they say in racing.

Springsteen ostentatiously looked over his shoulder and with a gesture visible everywhere in the infield, whacked open the throttle and simply left the Ducati in the dust.

Netz jumped up, shouted "Gotta call the office!" and sprinted for the nearest phone so he could tell all the folks back at the plant that the light had just come blazing out of the tunnel.

As it had. Next day in the BOT race, Adamo literally couldn't keep Springsteen in sight.

For the rest of the season O'Brien handed the BOT project over to

North Carolina dealer/tuner Don Tilley, who recruited a talented young dirt tracker named Gene Church to ride the series.

Just as useful, the newly formed Harley Owners' Group sponsored the effort, and Tilley and Church went on to take the series titles in 1983, '84, '85 and '86.

By that time, O'Brien had retired, or so he said. In fact, he was working as a consultant to several NASCAR teams, as well as H-D, and kept coming up with new improvements to the XR-1000 racing engine until there was nothing left to prove.

As noted elsewhere on these pages, the XR-1000 was not a sales success. And there's some debate over whether or not the project ever edged into the black.

Not only that, this chunk of racing history is a fine test of the adage, "Win on Sunday, Sell on Monday." They did, and it didn't.

But no one who followed Harley-Davidson's racing fortunes ever felt bad about that.

What all this adds up to was and is disappointment.

The *Cycle World* test quoted O'Brien as expecting buyers to flock to the showrooms. Evans says he was told the plan was to produce 200 a month for the 1983 model year.

Conner's much later data book shows 1,018 XR-1000s produced in 1983, 759 in model year 1984. Evans' figures are a guess of 1,400 in '83, followed by 752 for '84; 574 in the original slate gray, 176 in the newly optional black and orange, with one special paint job shipped to California.

The Motor Company declined to comment. A total of 1,800 for both model years is surely close. Evans reports that almost all the XR-1000s sold went for less than the original suggested retail price. And that there were bikes sitting in the dealerships as late as 1987.

At that point, just when Harley-Davidson was assured of survival and was on its way to becoming the American Icon H-D is now, human nature saved the day.

Repeating the saga of the XLCR, as soon as it became clear that the motorcycling public wasn't going to take to the XR-1000, the collectors did. The XR became a two-part club, with one chapter buying the bikes and restoring all the original parts and putting their machines on display, with extra points for the lowest numbers on the odometer.

The other chapter has worked out how to correct the weaknesses of the rocker arm bearings, the cases, and so forth. They ride their XRs long, hard, and fast, which has to come close to what the original project called for, even if—quoting Evans again—"They never made what we wanted."

So for the 1983 model year, working off the strength of the new frame and upgraded suspension and proven engine, as in the same parts for more than ten years, the XL model line got a new member.

There's a parallel happy accident here, in that the Johnson and Carter eras, the fuel crises, and so forth, had made the dollar bigger and the yen smaller, putting the prices of imports and domestics closer than they'd been for decades.

What this added up to was a bargain. The baseline Sportster, the lowest sticker price in the showroom, was called the XLX.

It was a stripper (a loss leader as they say in retail). It had the same XL engine used in the XLH and the XLS, which themselves differed only in details like size and shape of the fuel tank.

The XLX had the peanut tank, solo seat, low handlebars, and one front disc brake. The exhaust pipes were matte black, the body parts were glossy black, and chrome plating was kept to a minimum.

The suggested retail price was $3,995.

OK, that's not cheap. You could buy a wide variety of imports for less and some of them would have been faster and fancier.

But the XLX was a Harley-Davidson, at the very beginning of the fashion for Harleys, and the psychology was simply that the price gave buyers an excuse to buy Harley.

Next step in the sales chain was a reverse of previous policy. H-D used to make a profit on the basic package and offered the extras at the lowest possible price, as in $7.35 for custom paint as recently as 1971. And the choice of high or low bars, or exhaust pipes, was just that, a choice at no extra cost.

For 1983 H-D shifted to the car company's policy, with the low sticker and extras for, well, extra money. All the other parts would fit right on the XLX, so the buyer could get different colors, larger tanks, on through the catalog, while the sales force could either make the pitch on the bargain, or could move the prospect upscale.

There was more to its appeal than price, of course. The XLX was 15 pounds lighter than an XLH because it had the tiny seat and low bars. All the XLs by '83 came with the 16-inch rear wheel, which was the fashion by then even though it didn't provide as good a footprint. Other options—same price in this instance—were laced or cast wheels.

The XLX was a marketing move, with a solo seat, no tachometer and the choice of black paint. A balance tube had joined the exhaust pipes, which reduced noise and allowed the return of the now-classic hamcan air cleaner.

The laced wheels were the vogue, surely because motorcycles had spokes long after cars went to dull and boring stamping except for sports cars.

The cast wheels were (and are) heavier. And they were stiffer, which allows the suspension to work, flexing between the resistant frame and wheels.

Plus—and this applies to all makes and models—the cast wheels come with tubeless tires.

This is a safety issue. The old-style tires are held on the rim by the tube, under pressure. If a tube blows, the tire comes loose and flops and it's the scariest experience any rider will ever have. Just ask anyone who's been in the fast lane with the grips slapping the tank and the semi 50 yards back blowing his horn to let you know he's not sure he can stop in time.

A loss of pressure with the tubeless tire means a soft wobble, so the rider can sense the problem and find it and ride home slowly, stopping at the free pump if needed.

Not much of a decision—not if you've been there—but suffice it for now that tubeless is best.

Back with the XLX, the factory in mid-1984 chose to replace the generator with an alternator, which cranks out more juice, is less likely to fail, and weighs less. It also has the added bonus of putting an oil filter where the generator used to be.

(The XR-1000, incidentally, retained the generator because the engineers had more than enough to do with the new cases and so forth.)

Cycle World weighed the XLX with half a tank of fuel and reported 475 pounds, the lightest Sportster since the honest test was invented.

The test bike did the quarter-mile in 13.88 seconds, so the '84 XLX was lighter and quicker than the 1962 XLCH, which wasn't weighed down by electric start or hampered by emissions rules. OK, the four-cylinder imports were now rulers of the street, but even so, to be faster, lighter, safer, and cleaner all at once is no mean feat.

Like the XLCR before it, the XR1000 wasn't a huge hit when new but is now prized by collectors.
Jeff Hackett

Science has yet to devise an objective test for handling. But because suspension and frame and tire technology has come a long way over the past 40 years, it's safe to bet that the '84 XLX also handled better, as in more control, than the '62 XLCH could offer.

What we do know is that the *CW* testers were impressed with the nimble and predictable handling of the XLX. No weave, no wobble, and the agility meant a determined rider could match the pace of those on machines that on paper had more performance.

The business office's bottom line was that in 1983 the XLX was Harley-Davidson's best seller. Well sure it also had the lowest price, but that hasn't always been the case in H-D history.

Nor was it a runaway victory, not with 4,892 XLX sales vs. 3,277 for the Low Rider and 2,873 for the Wide Glide, both members of the Super Glide family and both with substantially higher sticker prices.

There's been some historical debate about this. Former H-D employees have suggested that while the

Like Levitra, the XLX got Harley back in the game.

XLX sold out and the XR-1000 just sat there, the high markup on the latter model and the loss leader role of the XLX meant that H-D collected as much money from the XR as it did from the XLX.

It could have happened that way.

But XRs were seen sitting on the showroom floor, costing the dealer interest on the money he borrowed to buy his stock. So if the factory made a profit it was done at the dealers' expense, a poor route to black ink.

It's also possible that the race success of the XR-1000, well, what the rules allowed the factory team to pretend its winner was, inspired prospects to visit their Harley store and check out the stock.

If this happened, as The Motor Company has hinted, and the XLX program brought in a lot of converts from the imports, then even if the racing fans walked in to see the XR-1000, they rode out on an XLX.

Now nearly a quarter of a century old, the XR1000 is still a handsome bike today.
Jeff Hackett

CHAPTER EIGHT

COMES THE EVOLUTION: 1986

Though still using the iron XL engine, the XLX set the pattern for all future Sportsters.

The XLX represented the Sportster's future, but it did so by reaching to its past.

The all-steel 1982 frame was retained, with some changes to the engine mounts but not much to the various dimensions. There was the single front disc brake, the alternator, and a diaphragm-spring clutch carried over from the previous XL-1000.

The configuration, as in the 45-degree included angle, had cylinders directly fore and aft, fork and blade connecting rods, four one-lobe camshafts in an arc in what H-D folks call the gearcase on the right side and chain primary on the left side.

The middleweight Harley engine got the four-cam design back in 1929, was revived in 1932, given recirculating oiling in 1937, gained unit construction in 1952, and got overhead valves, in 1952.

But the configuration and the outline had been the same all that time, and they didn't want to lose the look, or the character. And anyway, it's a perfectly valid way to build a motorcycle engine.

Within that parameter, as we say now, almost everything was different.

As a subtle sort of improvement, the flywheels and the mainshafts—the one on the left drives the engine sprocket and thus powers the primary drive to the gearbox, while the mainshaft on the right drives the cams, the ignition, and the oil pump—were forged as one piece, OK, a pair of pieces.

In the earlier engines, the shafts and flywheels were cast separately and then pressed together on a jig, which worked well enough in its day but always allowed some misalignment, which eventually wore out the bearings.

It's always better to make one piece and carve away until it's perfect than it is to press two parts together and hope they stay put.

Another internal change was the addition of hydraulic valve lifters.

This was sort of odd, in that the big Harley twins got hydraulic lifters back in the 1940s, when car engines were still using solid lifters, one of the few times H-D can claim to have been ahead of the art's

Late in 1985, The Motor Company made an announcement as close to no surprise as any new model unveiling has ever been.

For model year 1986 there would be an Evolution Sportster.

This was absolutely in context. More or less in order, Harley-Davidson had been bought from AMF by H-D's execs, some members of the founding families and a handful of other insiders. They'd borrowed all they could and then there'd been a couple of days when no one was sure the doors would open, but hard work, a thriving economy, and the timely arrival of a fashion for Harleys combined to keep the firm afloat, albeit in a sea of red ink.

Then the money started coming in. Investments in products like the FLT and FXR, the isolated-mount drivetrains for the big twin families, paid off and engineers finished meeting the federal government's demands. More important, there was talent and funding to take what clearly was the Sportster's next step forward.

Also in keeping with company policy and history, the step was larger than it looked.

state. And to be fair, the old system, with the owner or mechanic using a pair of wrenches to set the clearance by hand and feel, worked, and gave no trouble and had fewer parts.

But now, with government rules getting stricter by the year, and noise becoming a factor in the rules, the hydraulic lifters were preferred, both for quietness and ease of maintenance.

The major move, though, was aluminum cylinders and heads.

Also as noted, the big twins got alloy heads with the Panhead of 1948, but there were some difficulties with the techniques needed to cast alloy, much more difficult than solid ol' iron, and the engineers voted to keep iron when the XL engine was being designed.

Cast iron worked, as we've seen, but once again, time had either caught up or run out.

Above: *Simplicity defined the XLX.*

Left: *Black pipes looked mean.*

By 1983, when the XLX appeared, the Ironhead XL engine struggled to meet emissions standards.

Aluminum alloy brought two easy advantages. One, it sheds heat quicker and better than iron and two, it's lighter.

Assuming H-D and the firm's suppliers now knew how to work with alloy, which for the most part they did, those two factors would have been enough to justify the move. Aluminum does cost more than iron but in the modern economy, the cost of raw materials is much less a factor than items like meeting regulations and funding pensions and health insurance, so that cost wouldn't have mattered much.

There was more, though. This is something libertarians don't like to discuss but the fact is all those odious regulations about emissions and economy and noise did inspire and compel a lot of research, which paid off.

Motor industry engineers (never mind racing tuners) made major improvements in design. When gas got more expensive and less efficient, the engineers learned how to raise compression ratios despite lower octane ratings. There were major strides in combustion chamber and port designs, better control over fuel

Instrumentation consisted of a speedo—who needed a tach when the power curve was flat?

mixture and spark control, all of which meant more power from less fuel at lower levels of stress.

To illustrate, check the cylinder heads designs of the iron XL engine of 1957 and the alloy Shovelhead of 1966. They're close relatives if not twins.

But the Evolution FL-series engine of 1984 was radically different.

Not in configuration, we've had that discussion already. But the ports and chambers and valve angles and locations were all new and improved.

The hemispherical combustion chamber, as seen in racing engines as well as the 1936 Model E Knucklehead and the Chrysler V-8 of 1951, was a good

XLX suspension was hardly state of the art, even by 1983 standards.

Other than an electric starter and a displacement increase, not much had happened in the Sportster's engine bay since 1957.

design for the octane ratings and compression chambers of those days. But as the compression ratio went up, so did piston domes, converting the hemi head into an orange-peel head, which wasn't nearly as good.

All of which is background for the Evo XL's top end, which carried on the advances of the Evo FL.

The combustion chamber was (approximately) shaped like a bathtub, with smaller valves set at shallower angles. But because the actual combustion was better controlled, the compression ratio was 9:1, compared with the 8:1 to which the old ironhead had been reduced.

The headline here was that the Evo's bore and stroke had been returned to the 3.0 x 3.81-inches of the 1957 XL, 883-cc as they said then and we say now. This was a marketing move and a hint the press missed in '86. But because the engine was more efficient and the valve action under closer control, the camshaft timing and duration was milder. So the engine gained low-end power rather than needing to be buzzed up to the red line.

The Evo 883 was rated at 54 bhp at the output sprocket, or 42 bhp at the rear wheel, as compared with 50 bhp at the output sprocket from the ironhead's last version.

There were also advances in quality control, we were told, so the parts would fit together with less handwork.

And there were fewer parts; 426 for the new engine, 455 for the old version. And 206 of the 426 parts were new. They never did furnish a list or explain how one new part did the work of two or three old ones, sorry to say.

At $3995, the XLX was a bargain, at least by Harley standards.

The 1986 Sportster 883 was the most revolutionary model in Sportster history.

The new cylinder heads looked the newest, because they were.

And it wasn't just the internals that were new. The factory described this backwards, saying the rocker boxes were now made as a three-piece sandwich: you took off the top, then the center with the bolts, and then the section that carried the rocker arms. You could do it, they said, and service the top end without taking the engine out of the frame.

Which was true. What the factory bulletin left out was that the new engine was taller than the old version.

H-D had a new frame factory and could control quality at a lower cost, and so forth, but they hadn't wanted to change the Sportster frame much. With the old engine you could remove the one-piece rocker box, then the head, and the cylinder, all with the engine in place.

Now the top was bigger and higher so the rocker box had to be dismantled to do the same work. It's a minor point, but for those of us who've worked on both engines, details like that are important.

The sandwich used a set of rubber, more likely rubberlike, gaskets, rather than the old glue-on fiber

type Another advance when it worked right, and another hint at what the future would hold.

For the record, the Evo XL had triple-row chain primary drive, #530 chain final drive, four speeds forward in a cassette-style transmission, a single disc brake in front and single disc brake in the rear, 18-inch and 19-inch cast wheels, classic one-inch H-D handlebars, 12-volt electric's with electronic ignition, dry sump oil system with a three-quart tank and a really useful drain. It was basically a short piece of hose, which the owner could unclamp and aim at the drain pan, the easiest oil change in motoring history.

The carburetor came from Keihin, 34 mm in diameter with a butterfly throttle valve and an acceler-

ator pump, and with the classic Hamcan air cleaner still in service.

At this point The Motor Company made an investment in its future.

The ironhead XLX began life priced at $3,995, sold well and may have kept the company going. But the 1985 XLX was priced at $4,695, presumably because of inflation.

Imagine the surprise and delight of the public, then, when the company said the sticker price for the Evo XLH-883 would be . . . $3,995.

Yes. Arguably the most important revision/improvement in the Sportster line since the introduction of the OHV engine. And the price was less than it

With its aluminum engine, the new 883 was a Sportster for people who didn't know how to overhaul their bike on the side of the road with nothing but an adjustable wrench and a Zippo lighter for tools.

had been for a clearly inferior (well, mostly, but that will be seen in due course) predecessor.

There was also a new arrangement of the models and options. The levels, as in XLX and then the XLH Sportster and XLS Roadster, plus the Hugger suspension and seat, were no longer in the catalog.

Everyone then and since had referred to the baseline Evo 883 as an XLX and that's what it looked like, with black paint, solo seat, low bars, peanut tank, and a minimum of chrome plating. But the designation was XLH-883.

Then came upgrades, with a dual seat, passenger pegs, higher bars, larger tank, other paint schemes and so forth, but these were options. $25 for passenger pegs, $75 for red paint, $85 for the thicker and more comfy seat, on down the list.

Getting ahead of history a bit here, several months into the model year there came the XLH-1100,

Above: *The 883 retained the simplicity of the XLX*. Right: *In 1991 the Sportster received a five-speed transmission.*

the Evo engine with the bore increased from 3.0 to 3.35-inches, and with larger valves and ports. Similar to the original XL and XLH, or even how the 61-cid E Model became the 74-cid F engine.

We can make some reasonably accurate comparisons between the XLX-1000 and the XLH-883.

Both used the all-steel frame and shared suspension components and the single disc brakes front and rear and the small seat and tank. Both had a nominal 60-inch wheelbase and 30-inch seat height, 19-inch front wheel and 16-in. rear.

Cycle magazine tested the new 883 and found it weighed 477.5 pounds with the tank filled. *Cycle World* did its tests with the tank half full on the logical grounds that one can't ride a motorcycle with the tank full or empty so there's no reason to weigh them that way. *Cycle World*'s 1984 test of the XLX lists a weight of 475 pounds.

Gasoline officially weighs 6 pounds/gallon. So, 6 x 1.12=6.72 + 475=481, oh, round it off to 482 pounds for the XLX in *Cycle*'s trim, call it 6 pounds lighter for the Evo model, and that squares with the factory's

Though not as fast as the 1000cc Ironhead Sportster it replaced, the 883 was a solid performer.

In 1991 the Sportster also received a belt final drive system.

claim that the new engine was 8.2 pounds lighter than the old version.

Still comparing, the last iron XLs used electronic ignition, which provided a more carefully tailored advance curve and allowed the compression ratio to be raised from the nominal 8:1 of the '83 to 8.8:1.

This gives us two sides of an issue. Remember, the Evo 883 was rated at less bhp than the 1000 engine in its final tune.

The engines shared a relatively long stroke, which dictated a relatively low redline and both had a rev limit set at 6,000 rpm built into the ignition.

The two machines shared a 16-inch cast rear wheel and even came with the same tire, a Dunlop MT90-16.

The subtle difference here was that the 883 could be built with more quality control, was made of better material and the design of the valves and ports and combustion chambers gave better breathing and thus were more efficient. The design engineers said the 883 was a better engine because it could do the same work with less stress. That is, the alloy engine had 12 percent less displacement while giving away only 9 percent less peak torque. Ratings were a claimed 44 ft-lb for the 883 vs. 55 ft-lb for the 1000, both at 4,000 rpm.

As a slight offset here, the 883 was a smoother engine all the way up and down the rev scale. So the new model's final drive gearing was 3.98:1, while the '85 XLX pulled 3.79:1.

Why all this detail here? Because in plain test terms, the clearly improved XLH-883 wasn't quite as quick as the now obsolete iron XLX.

One of the tester's first lessons in reality comes with the realization that the facts in the brochure don't always match the numbers on the clocks. For instance the weights of the Sportster models over the years aren't always what the specs would have predicted.

The second lesson is that the impression, how the test rider feels about the performance of the machine, isn't always reflected or justified by the test results.

Case in point is that *Cycle* and *Cycle World* were both staffed by honest and competent riders. The methods varied, also a point on which debate can be honest. Even so, the two can be fairly compared.

Cycle's XLH-883 turned the standing quarter-mile in 14.37 seconds with a trap speed of 85.80 mph. The average fuel consumption during the test period was 54 mpg.

Cycle World's XLX did the quarter-mile in 13.88 seconds, with a trap speed of 93.75 mph. The test loop showed 60 mpg, while the test records showed 58 mpg.

What we actually had here was a test of the old adage about there being no substitute for cubic inches.

Quoting *Cycle*'s test again, "In all likelihood, even longtime Sportster riders won't miss the power, but

Tank graphics announced the extra cog in the transmission.

everyone who's ever slung a leg over an old-style XL will at once see the improvements in the Evolution bike."

The magazine went on to say that the delivery of torque, the effectiveness of the gearing, and the Evo's being quieter and smoother at all road and engine speeds meant that the new model didn't feel slow at all.

(We'll skip over another factor, that H-D knew when the 883 was announced that within the model year's span there would be an upgrade, the 1100 Evo.)

What mattered at the time was yet another historical quirk.

Back when Harley's engineers and planners decided their potential buyers wouldn't settle for an XR-750 detuned to meet the federal regs, Yamaha voted the other way by introducing a shaft-drive 750 twin that wasn't fast but mimicked the homemade choppers. It had a stepped seat, high bars, and a riding posture that felt totally cool at the stoplight. Never mind that half an hour was the normal rider's limit in the saddle.

They called it a custom. Several had tried at copying the homemade Harleys seen in the movies. H-D's own Super Glide did the job and became a big seller, while the ape-hangered Norton and Kawasaki versions sank without a trace (thank goodness).

But the Yamaha sold and the market shifted and the other big factories began edging into the mid-size twin niche, replacing the long-gone English machines. And my point is?

There was a useful economic trend here, with the dollar/yen balance shifting and making it possible for a Harley, the Evo 883, to compete on price, undercutting Honda's 1100 Shadow by $200 and Yamaha's 920 Virago by $500, just as it weighed less than Honda's 700 Shadow.

The point here is, just as the larger import makers moved into Harley territory, Harley-Davidson introduced a model that could compete as a motorcycle, dollar for dollar, pound for pound, and even on the basis of quality control.

This was a milestone motorcycle, and must be ranked with the 1936 Knucklehead and above the Electra-Glide of 1965 or the Super Glide of 1971.

Meanwhile, back with the first impressions of 1986, um, hang on here. To keep the historical perspective, it's noted here that the written portions of a test are relative, if not subjective. *Cycle World*'s test of the '68 XLH doesn't contain even the word "vibration." The closest the test report comes is to say the bike can be ridden "for an hour, little more" while not explaining the limit. In 1965, *CW* said "The Sportster is quite a comfortable motorcycle," while the gearbox "shifts with remarkable precision and smoothness."

So here's *Cycle* in 1986, saying the Evo's "four-speed gearbox serves adequately but we were less than pleased with the shift action."

Not only that, the Evo test reported "the 883 feels perceptibly smoother than the older models—vibration never becomes intolerable—even at its worst the new 883 never approaches the bothersome vibration level of the Sportsters we've tried in recent years."

The engine and gearbox were pretty much the same between 1965 and 1985. What had changed was the rest of the world. That is, when all motorcycles numbed the hands and loosened the fillings, no one bothered to say so.

This isn't to find fault with the earlier tests or the guys who wrote them. Instead, we need now to keep in mind that the standards of the day—change from day to day.

Even so, the Evo 883 made an excellent first impression. *Cycle* commented on the usual Harley quirks, as in the air cleaner intruding on the rider's legroom, the heat from the oil tank, and the odd position of the ignition key. (There was no mention of old stuff like the lack of steering head lock or a toolkit.)

The Public Goes Testing

The next traditional Motor Company event came in the first few months of sales.

The revised gearbox, or perhaps the shift mechanism, wasn't quite right and had a tendency to lock in gear, most often first, making for a long ride home.

There were some flaws in the cast wheels, which came from Australia of all places. They were replaced under warranty and, of course, the gearbox was fixed for free, too.

The hydraulic lifters sometimes lost pressure, refusing to fill and creating extra valve clearance while making a disquieting noise.

This wasn't a warranty thing, most of the time. Instead, what the new owners did was coast to a stop, let the engine sit for a minute or two, and restart. Almost always, the pressure came back.

The Evo XL engine was smoother and quieter and the dyno-test loss of power wasn't noticed on the road.

Proving I suppose that you can move from New England to California but you can't stop a Yankee from pinching pennies, I'd been riding for, gosh, 32 years before buying myself my first brand-new motorcycle.

This proved to be more difficult than I expected. My pick was (you guessed, of course) an Evo 883 and when I went to the nearest dealership in mid-model year, I was told all the basic 883s had been sold.

Ditto for the second-closest store, and the third and the fourth.

But then I arrived at Westminster H-D, Winchester, CA, and was met by a chap named Joe O'Day. All their 883s were gone, he said, then paused.

"We've got more coming," he said. "Leave me your name and phone number."

Maybe a week later, O'Day called. "Your Sportster is here."

What could I say? I hopped in my truck and drove to Westminster and paid the $3,995 and loaded the 883 in the truck and drove home.

Personal prejudice came into play here, and I know what the tests said (in fact I think I wrote one), but for myself, I couldn't bring myself to sit on that dumb little solo brick. But I'd already bought a Corbin Gunfighter seat—the accessory guys had worked this out early and were ready with improvements for the Evo XL—and I hate that balance tube in the exhaust so I got a Supertrapp 2-into-1, in stainless steel no less.

And months earlier I'd stumbled across a used gas tank, the 3.5-gallon Teardrop style first seen on the Aermacchi Sprint and then on the Super Glide and occasionally on the seldom-sold XLT. I bought it for $10 or so and tucked it under the workbench in anticipation of just what I'd planned to do.

Here's where thrift really paid dividends. I removed the front fender (easy) and the rear fender (tough because there's no plug-in connections and I had to weasel the wires through holes in the metal that were too small). I took the tank and fenders down to my local paint shop and had the bodywork painted Harley Racing Orange.

Bragging here, I paid $250 for the paint job, and got a color seen on no other Evo 883. I would have had to pay $300 for a color in the Harley catalog.

The teardrop tank, meanwhile, was virtually free and gave me a cruising range of 150 miles, instead of the 85-90–mile range with the peanut tank. And the seat was comfy and the pipes were music.

This chunk of history is presented here as illustration. I wasn't alone in this sort of project. In fact, I'd bet a couple thousand of the Evo 883 buyers did much the same thing, except with their own pick of paint and pipes and so forth.

This was, in my view, simply what real Harley guys did and had been doing since the sport models and the early modifieds, known then as cutdowns, hit the streets in the 1920s.

But wait, there's more.

I'd barely put the break-in miles on my 883 when the gearbox locked up, just as the factory had warned, half a block from home. It was fixed under warranty.

Then came the notice that the wheels were being recalled.

The 16-inch rear wheel has always looked wrong to me. Oh yeah, it's the fad and The Look, but the choice of tire was limited and the footprint shaped wrong for hard riding. So when the dealership called me in I asked, "Will the factory pay for an 18-inch rear wheel?"

"Yes," the dealer said, "but we don't know where you'll ever find one. They haven't been a stock item since 'way back in 1979."

"Ha!" I said. This is another old-timer rant, but when I was a lad the Harley-Davidson dealer prided himself on having the parts you'd need before you knew you needed 'em.

So I called Ol' Sherm down at Oceanside Harley-Davidson and sure enough he had a cast 18-inch Sportster rear wheel stashed in the shed behind the shop. The Motor Company paid him for it, and I paid for the new and better tire and it all went together without problem one.

(Now of course Sherm has retired and the dealership has moved to a swank new building and all their money is invested in T-shirts for dogs and lingerie for ladies and they've sold all their pre-Evo parts but they were kind enough to tell me who bought the stuff, which is all one can hope for.)

My 883's valves did pump down a couple of times but shutting the engine off, counting to a minute, and firing up again, worked.

Getting ahead of the narrative here, the alternator did collapse later (and a nasty noise it made, too). When the XL line got belt final drive, the factory issued a kit and I converted from chain to belt, again bolt-on stuff.

Here's another story I nearly forgot. When Harley went to belt final drive, the big twins got the first versions and the literature warned that you had to remove the swingarm to replace the belt, which scared me. When I decided the belt had enough miles on it, I went to the dealership, San Diego H-D in fact, but before I signed the papers the parts gal casually mentioned, you don't have to drop the swingarm on a Sportster, so I went home and did the job myself, easy-peasy.

At 40,000 miles or so, I decided the engine had to be tired. I went the 1200 route, as easy as new pistons and boring the cylinders to 3.5-inch. I kept the smaller 883 valves because I wanted torque more than peak power.

Finally, in 2001, I dropped in on the dealership to get some parts— a grommet for the side cover if memory serves—and there parked out front was an 883 in bright yellow with a cast 19-inch front wheel, low bars, all the stuff I wanted and none I disliked. So I barged into the sales office and asked, "Whuddalya gimme on my '86 with 93,000 miles on it?"

"$2,500," said Jerry and we had a deal. If any deal ever justified its original purpose, well, do the math. My Evo 883 cost me $100 per year, proving that I should have begun buying new 30 years before I did.

When the engines had some miles racked up, the alternators tended to come apart, something that can't be fixed at roadside, but it didn't happen to every bike.

There were some bad bolts used to hold the front brake caliper, resulting in another recall notice for obvious reasons.

And the records show three—yes three—tries at getting a battery cable that didn't stretch or vibrate itself to death. The number of fixes tells you how common this glitch was, with the salvation here being that when the scoot rolled to a stop all lights out and the engine dead, the canny owner could remove the seat—oh, that's if the canny owner had fitted a tool-bag below the headlight—and poke around until the broken cable revealed itself, and crimp it back together and yup it's the voice of experience here, the canny owner on that occasion being the author's son.

(Family joke: Several years after this, my two older sons sold their Harleys to go into business. Where did I fail? How did I go wrong?)

This litany of minor, for the most part, disaster isn't exactly a complaint. All new models manage to sneak flaws past the test procedures.

The good news and the historical value is that the Evo XL not only came at a good time, a time when the public had rediscovered motorcycles and when the price was right, but it came when H-D was building motorcycles that could compete on their merits. And the public knew it. Plus, they responded by voting with their wallets.

The Motor Company has always been willing to link its products with current or historical events. Witness deals on bikes for firefighters after 9/11. In 1986, there was a celebration of the anniversary of the Statue of Liberty, and H-D offered graphics and paint and certificates of ownership for Liberty Editions, for the big twins as well as for the XLH-1100. (Presumably because it was the starter model, there was no such treatment for the Evo 883.)

The records for the model run that year show 8,026 basic 883s, 2,322 with upgrades such as paint and tanks, 3,077 of the 1100s, plus 954 of the Liberty versions.

That's 14,379 Sportsters out the door. That's more than twice as many (6,514 according to Rick Conner) as the factory sold in the ironhead's last year, and the XLH was easily the best-selling Harley product.

Not only that, the Evo XL sales had to have been conquest sales.

First, there were buyers who'd discovered motorcycling, as the industry council phrases it.

Second, there were Sportster buyers who either had imports, or would have bought one except that the XL was more machine for the dollar and wasn't going to break down the way the earlier ones did, or were rumored to do.

What this all adds up to is simply the best, and the best-selling, and the most-needed sales and critical success, since the Knucklehead of 1936.

And that was just a start.

CHAPTER NINE

THE EXTENDED FAMILY: 1987-2003

Harley soon followed the XL883 with larger Sportster models.

By the late 1980s Harley was experiencing a phenomenal comeback, selling every Sportster it built.

One major reason Harley-Davidson's sales and engineering staff was willing to begin with the mild version of the Evo, the 883 that gave away displacement, power, and performance to the rival twins from, say, Honda and Yamaha, was that they'd read the script, flipped to the last page, and knew the happy ending, that within a few months the 883 would be joined by the XLH-1100.

The sales and engineering offices were both mentioned here because they had to be working in unison.

The 1100 engine came six weeks after the 883. It wasn't a major change. The 1100 had the bore increased from 3.0-inches to 3.35, and it had larger valves . . . and 10 more bhp.

This put the Evo XL into new territory. Now the alloy engine had more power (and displacement, don't forget) than the iron engine. It would edge the Honda twins in any impromptu contest of speed.

The 1100 only came as an upgrade, so to speak, with a tachometer, dual seat, higher bars, and a second mirror, with a choice of paint schemes. It was mostly the options offered for the 883, already fitted.

The puzzles are in the details. The original 1100 was a larger version of the 883, but with larger valves and ports.

For model year 1987, the 1100 came with a new cylinder head, which kept the 9:1 compression ratio of the earlier 1100, but was more of a hemi head. This at a

time when that configuration was declared outmoded. The semi-hemi, which also was fitted to the 883 in '87, had smaller parts and the engineers said the increase in intake velocity and cleaner burning combined to boost power by 5 percent, again in both versions of the engine.

The 1100's suggested retail price was $5,495, this against the basic 883's boost to $4,495. For that extra grand, the buyer got the fancy stuff—dual seat, higher bars, and choice of colors, tachometer, and other items—but also got more performance.

Cycle tested the '87 1100 and reported it was the quickest Harley on the market, with a 13.15 second quarter-mile, outsprinting last year's 883 and the new Low Rider Sport despite the latter's 80-cid V2 engine.

The 1100 lost to Honda's 1100 Shadow, a V-twin clearly aimed at the H-D buyer, at the drag strip. But on the road, rolling on full power from 40-70 mph, the Harley beat both the Honda and their mutual challenger, the Yamaha 1000 Virago.

Cycle reported 48 mpg during the test, with 53 mpg possible cruising at the legal limit.

The measured seat height was 29 inches, a figure to be commented on shortly, while *Cycle*'s crew said the low seat was useful in slow-speed maneuvers.

Contradicting earlier comments, the test reported the 1100's "long-range ability is twice cursed, by a hard saddle and intense vibration in the 55-70 mph speed range."

Peanut tank, Hamcan air cleaner, KR low pipes . . . it's hard to notice the Evo engine of the belt final drive.

The XL1100 and later XL1200 proved strong performers.

Even so, they said, "The Sportster remains a machine that demands the rider conform to its elemental approach. Harley has built Sportsters this way for 30 years, and they sell: currently the Sportsters . . . constitute Harley's best-selling model line, for reasons beyond history, appearance, sound, and image."

The Real Hugger

What the editors at *Cycle* meant by that comment, they didn't say. But the second puzzle dropped its first shovel with the 1100 test panel, showing the 1100 weighing 474.5 pounds with full tanks, 109 pounds less than Honda's 1100 and plainly one reason for the win in the roll-on contest.

Through it all the Sportster series retained its graceful beauty.

Then came the '87 Hugger.

Kudos to *Cycle* here, in large part because they mentioned that the model was supposed to appeal to women, something H-D never had the, um, huevos to admit in public.

The original Hugger arrived back in 1979, recall, with the seat height lowered by the simple expedients of shorter shock absorbers and a thinner seat.

The '80 (model year) version used the old iron engine, of course, and came when new buyers were rare. There weren't many Huggers sold, which is why it took nearly 10 years, and new management, to bring the idea back, new and improved, as they say.

Sounds odd, but the Hugger Redux got most of its height reduction from an old motocross trick. The Hugger's swingarm mounted the lower end of the shocks further back, lay-down shocks as the dirt guys called it. This lowered the frame, while the angle provided a rising-rate spring. That is, the ride would be soft on little bumps, firmer as the impact increased. Neat, eh? And the factory got to use the same shocks for all the XLs, which we're told kept the price down

In 1994 the top-of-the-line Sportster was the XL1200 Deluxe.

'cause the supplier could design and build all the shocks to one spec.

Next, the Hugger came as a lowered, basic XL883, with the solo seat and peanut tank, one front disc brake and no tachometer, but with buckhorn bars, the semi-custom bend that put the grips closer to the rider.

But the Hugger's solo seat had a different cover, filler material, and shape. And it had more padding in the back and less on the sides, putting less distance between the rider's butt and the ground.

With that, you got questionable marketing. H-D's promotional folks somehow decided to measure seat

A rider from 1959 would still recognize the distinct profile of a modern Sportster.

For 1996 Harley put the "sport" back in Sportster, with the XL1200S.

height with a 180-pound rider on board, as in "No Dear those leather pants don't make you look fat . . ."

With seat and filler and shocks compressed, the Hugger's official seat height was 26.75 inches That was still higher than the imported rival twins and was an inch or so lower than the static, unladen measurement used by other makers and the magazines.

Other than that, the '87 Hugger was an 883, so it did the same times and mpg (53.8 average for *Cycle*'s

test), was offered for $200 more than the basic XLH, oh heck speaking of marketing, the retail price of the plain 883 was $4495 that year, but for 1988 they dropped it back to $3995, with the Hugger at $4199. Imagine how the buyers of the '87s felt about that.

Cycle found the 883 to vibrate nearly as much as the 1100, except that the worst buzz came at 65 mph. That was odd, as the two engines came with the same final drive gearing.

And for a second puzzle, the wet weight for the Hugger, same magazine standards, same time frame and scale, same issue even, was 478.5 pounds.

So it picked up four pounds from moving the shocks and repacking the seat? How can that be? What it really does is remind us of what the magazine guys have always said: We don't know the answers, all we can do is report the results.

The final '87 model news was some anniversary editions.

Mark the plural. There was an anniversary paint treatment for the FLHTC, and a 10th Anniversary treatment for the Low Rider version of the Super Glide. And 600 (according to factory figures) XLH-1100s got decals and trim celebrating the Sportster's 30th year.

The XL1200S was the fastest bike in Harley's 1996 lineup.

The S wasn't just about speed—top-notch suspension made it handle, too.

The S was the first Sportster to feature an adjustable front fork.

(As sort of a parallel puzzle, H-D has been doing these treatments for at least 25 years. Most are seldom if ever seen in public again. Where do you suppose they go?)

The Full 1200

The 1988 model show brought some real news. The 1100 version of the XL engine was replaced by the 1,200-cc edition. It was easily done, with the bore increased from 3.35 to 3.5 inches. The larger engine got heads with larger combustion chambers, to keep the compression ratio compatible with the low-octane stuff dictated by the government, and with valves and ports sized to match the engine's added displacement.

This was a sensible move, predictable even because the FL family began as a 61, metrically a 1,000-cc engine, and grew into the now classic 74, or 1,200-cc. It was almost genetic, then, for the XL to grow from 883cc to 1,000, then back to 883 and then to 1,200.

As a mark of our changing world, meanwhile, back in the old days the engines were called 45s or 61s or 74s. The metric notion was a long way off, in time and distance.

Now we have a mix, as in we're all used to 250s, or 600s, and so on up the scale, but nobody in the Harley factory or outside has ever referred to the XLH-1200 as a 74.

More important, the 1200 was a clear improvement. The '88 XLH-1200 engine produced 75 bhp at the output sprocket and, yes, that's 5 bhp more than the ill-fated XR-1000, and it's nearly twice the output of the first Evo 883.

This put the Sportster back into the (two-cylinder) performance market. The stock 1200 could turn the quarter-mile in 13 seconds flat, a match for the imports and easily quicker than any car you'd meet in daily life. As another benefit, the XLH-1200 was a shade quicker and faster than the sports version of the FX line. The paperboy's bike had become the toughest kid in the family, pause for gloating chuckle.

A talented rider could put the S model's high-grade suspension to good use.

In addition to the sporty S model, Harley introduced the chopperesque XL1200C.

Did we mention earlier that Harley-Davidson entered the accessory business years ago? True, for all manner of extras.

With the 1200 model came another sort of it. The dealers offered conversions, pistons to allow the 883 barrels to be bored out—the design had anticipated this, not incidentally—and the larger pistons fitted. They were dished, so the compression ratio remained the same, and with the added size came a factory claim of 70 bhp.

The 1200 kit had less peak power because it had the smaller valves. While it gave more punch at the low end, it worked exceptionally well at moderate speeds. All the 883 owner had to do was ride the stock engine until it needed work, 40,000 miles in this reporter's case, and have the kit installed and go another 50,000 miles with extra power, as your humble scribe did.

The Family

No one thought about this at the time, but the Sportster had evolved in more ways than one. There was the basic 883, the Hugger version of same, the upscale 883, and the 1200, which came stock with the 883's extras—dual seat, buckhorn bars, laced-spoke wheels, and so forth.

HAPPY ANNIVERSARY

There's a little switch here, made because of research, or perhaps clever promotional work, but those with a memory for obscure facts will recall that Harley-Davidson celebrated its 50th Year in 1954.

True. And then, the 75th was observed in 1978, the 85th in 1988, the 95th in 1998, and in 2003 H-D threw a tremendous party in Milwaukee (and the surrounding area because downtown Milwaukee wasn't big enough for the several hundred thousand Harley fans, owners, and their families who attended the parties, parades, and concerts held in late August and early September that year).

The switch in anniversary dates is a subject about which Harley-Davidson officials and staff will say and have said nothing.

A (very) independent researcher and Harley fan, Herbert Wagner, became intrigued by the question and spent several years checking all the newspapers and magazines of the early twentieth century, looking for how and when Harley-Davidson first appeared.

It's his surmise that Harley and the Davidson brothers actually completed their first true motorcycle in 1904, but that during the promotional battles of the pioneer years Harley advocates as well as Indian partisans and believers in Thor, Ivor-Johnson, Excelsior, and peers, fudged the facts about who was there first.

Then, later, Harley-Davidson's founders refused to criticize the advertising guys who'd overdone the claims, so the error became the official history.

Or so Wagner claimed in his book, *At The Creation* (University of Wisconsin Press), which appeared in time for the 100th party.

And no one paid much attention. Strike that, what happened was, everyone had a wonderful time at the celebration, even those who went home early when Elton John turned out to be the surprise guest.

What we have here is a classic case of legend outrunning fact. All Model T Fords weren't black,* you can't see the Great Wall of China from outer space, and George Washington couldn't have thrown a silver dollar across the Potomac because there weren't any silver dollars when he was a kid.

But those legends remain, no matter what. And so will Harley-Davidson's birth year remain 1903, no matter what. Nor will anyone be harmed in the making of the legend.

Meanwhile, H-D and the motorcycle world were getting ready for some changes.

The Evo XL was getting a bit long in the tooth, as the horse traders phrase it.

Cycle World assigned the 883C to a retro comparison test in 2001, grouped with Kawasaki's 800-cc liquid-cooled V-twin that was a frank copy of an Indian Chief, the reborn Triumph Bonneville from the revived company of that name, and the Kawasaki W650, a revival of that maker's earlier vertical twin that in turn was a cheerful copy of a BSA.

The Sportster didn't do very well. *Cycle World* was running all test bikes on the chassis dynamometer and the 883C, at 43.1 bhp, was the least powerful of the group.

The 883C was second heaviest, and the slowest on the drag strip, and tied for the lowest top speed. It gave the best mileage of the group, and the new tank provided a cruising range equal to the bikes with larger tanks.

The *CW* guys in the group were all sports-minded riders, so it was no surprise that they didn't care for the awkward riding position, the forward controls or the awkward low-speed flop of the 21-inch front wheel.

Still, they concluded, the Sportster won the Authenticity Trophy as the only machine in the crowd that really was what it claimed to be, with a genuine bloodline going all the way back to its origins.

And at least two members of the test panel wondered out loud if a standard 1200 wouldn't have been just as retro, in its way, while winning the comparison.

For the bottom line and closure for an era, and a hint, not that one is needed, "Vibration? Yes, there's more than the other three bikes featured here, and the 883 ain't much of an interstate cruiser. Above 70 mph grip vibration can make your palms feel as if they're being nibbled by ducks."

Stay tuned.

*Henry Ford offered a choice of color when production began, but black was the only paint that would dry as fast as the production line moved, so Ford efficiently dropped the grays and greens. You could look it up.

Custom touches on the C included higher bars, 21-inch front tire, and fatter tank.

In effect, this was a platform, with a choice of parts and prices ranging from $3,995 to $5,875, and with the option of getting the 1200 engine with a solo seat, in basic black, or an 883 in vivid color.

Then H-D began to expand, widen, and improve the Sportster group. And there was an accidental prediction. Back when the Evo 883 arrived, *Cycle* commented that it was odd to see this work being done on the XL while elsewhere H-D was doing radical changes, for instance belt drive and isolated drivetrains.

Guess what?

The '88s got larger fork tubes, up to 39 mm from 35 mm, longer shock absorbers, a longer swingarm, and a 40-mm CV Keihin carburetor. The later 883s were rated at 45 bhp, against the factory's claim of 42 bhp for the first ones.

In 1989, the factory did some minor adjustments. It added an alloy intake manifold, new air cleaner element, and offset wrist pins for the pistons to reduce rocking forces on the bores. The XLs were basically carryovers for 1990.

The Belt Way

The '91 Sportsters had all the new that's fit to print.

Belt drive was, of course, a pioneer feature, as seen on the Harleys of 1904 through 1914. These belts served as a clutch before the clutch was invented.

But when Harley-Davidson re-invented belt drive for the 1980 Sturgis, the material was space-age polymers and so forth. They were chosen because the best were cleaner, quieter, more durable, and needed less maintenance than the conventional chain. By the way, none of the critics who said Harley-Davidson didn't innovate spoke up when H-D did just that. Belt final drive proved useful and practical and was added to the other Harley models as money and availability permitted. The belt reached the Sportster family in '91, mostly. The belt was standard for the 1200 and the upgraded 883, while the basic 883 kept the chain.

The Motor Company kept to its traditions, too. Along with the belt drive for the fancier new XLs, the dealers could stock a kit, with new notched sprockets, spacers, and so forth, to convert older, well, older Evo XLs, to belt drive.

Once again, this was a good move. Owners simply waited until the chain needed to be replaced, and bit the one-time bullet. The belt kit cost several times

Harley's two new 1996 Sportsters, the C and the S.

cassette. That is, the shafts, gears, shifter mechanism, and so on are installed, serviced, and removed as a unit. All the engineers had to do was put five sets of gears on the two shafts, in the space formerly occupied by four sets of gears. Once metallurgy and production quality could do that with some hope of long-lived gears, it wasn't a tough change to make.

The minor drawback here was that the XL engine doesn't like being buzzed. It's a long stroke and the narrow V-twin is inherently out of balance—always has been. So the higher it's revved, the more it vibrates. Winding it past its power peak gets nothing.

At the same time, the motorcycle owner expects to click into top gear and cruise the highway. So the planners know the engine has to rev high enough to produce enough power to push the bike up any grade on the interstate, two-up, even in windy weather.

Put this all together and the final drive gearing of a 5-speed XL isn't all that much taller than the ratio of the 4-speed XL. It's 4.22:1 for an iron 1000, 3.98:1 for an Evo 883, 3.61:1 for an 883 Evo with 5-speed.

What this comes to in the real world is that an Evo 883 will cruise the highway, in comfort with minimum buzz, at 70-75 mph. This is so with the 4-speed, or the 5-speed, which are only a few hundred rpm apart.

What the 5-speed does is allow a lower low, and a higher high, so there is an improved launch and a one mpg or so improvement.

What the 5-speed buyer really gets is improved perception. Lots of 5-speeds are racy; competition bikes need the gears 'cause they have narrow power bands, one thing the XL has never been accused of. So the public assumes five speeds are better than four, which is why H-D put the 5-Speed labels where folks couldn't miss 'em.

The good/bad news here is that when the gearbox cavity was being repacked, the shift mechanism was revised and changes made to the engine's lower end, which means there is no retrofit. So there's no 5-speed conversion possible for the older 4-speed Evo XLs.

Handlebar design on the C imitated the design of the FXLR Low Rider.

what a chain did, but once done the bike was quieter and vibrated less and didn't need lubing every couple hundred miles and, in your reporter's case, the new belt lasted 50,000 miles.

The other big leap for '91 was five speeds for the gearbox. This wasn't quite the benefit it was expected to be. The basics were simple, though, in that the XL gearbox was two shafts, installed as what's known as a

(Later, the aftermarket came up with a 6-speed conversion for the 5-speed models, a true overdrive to raise the comfort level to 75-80 mph . . . and cost several thousand dollars, speaking of good/bad news.)

These major improvements were followed by breathing room. For 1992, the chain-drive XLs got an o-ring chain, and the Hugger was lowered another 1.5 inches and given the name Super Hugger, to which no one outside the ad agency paid any attention.

In 1993 all the Sportsters got the belt final drive, a logical move as 1) the belt is better than the chain and 2) this reduces the number of parts the dealer is supposed to have on hand.

Harley-Davidson celebrated its 90th anniversary in 1993, so the company built 1,993 (get it?) XL1200s with serialized nameplate, special emblems and badges, and two-tone paint, silver and charcoal satin. Everything else about the 90th XLs was stock.

The C proved more popular than the S.

Instrumentation of the C remained basic.

Next page: Government-mandated mirrors looked out of place on the trick C model.

There was a corporate policy change in 1992 and The Motor Company no longer reported the numbers of models sold per year. So we don't know how many of the anniversary models were actually built or sold.

The XL frame was revised at the rear in 1994. The clutch cable got a quick-release connection, so you no longer had to remove the primary drive cover to replace the cable. The forks for the 883s were improved by fitting the stiffer top triple clamp already used on the 1200s. The press wasn't told they were different until they no longer were, by the way.

Meeting New Demands

At this point in the company's history, the hard times were, well, history. H-D had become famous as an American success story, thriving in the market and on the stock market. Some part of this has to have been (and still is) the company's skill at creating and analyzing what the buyers want, sometimes before the buyers know.

During the same time, there were some changes in reporting and testing, which makes comparison a bit more difficult. For example, the factory listed the XLH1200 engine's output as 71 crankshaft bhp. That

is, power measured at the engine's sprocket, before reaching the primary drive, clutch, gearbox, final drive, and pavement. The '95 1200 models came with an enlarged peanut tank, same shape but containing 3.3 gallons rather than 2.3. The factory said the machine's dry weight was 490 pounds. The 883s were listed as 488 pounds for the basic, 485 for the Hugger, perhaps because the 883s came with the smaller tank and the shorter version has less, what? Shock absorber weight? The magazines, meanwhile, found all the Sportsters topping 500 pounds, ready for the road.

Next, sales appeal. According to *American Demographics* magazine, the average motorcycle owner in 1980 was 27 years old. In 1988, the average owner was 38 years old. It's safe to guess the average owner earned more money and took fewer chances.

In short, the market had changed and diversified. There were lots of young guys buying sport bikes, the quick and nimble imported multis. But the major share was going to what had become known as cruisers, typically identified by high handlebars, stepped seats, forward controls, chrome plate slathered everyplace except the tires, and a riding posture that cracks the rider's back after half an hour (yes, I overstated).

Which is futile. The thing to do is what Harley-Davidson did in 1996.

There were two models that year.

One was the XL1200C, for Custom, another way of saying cruiser. The 1200C had a 21-inch front wire wheel and 16-inch disc rear wheel, engine trim in chrome and black, stepped dual seat, and a claimed seat height of 27.1 inches. (Same as that year's Hugger, by the way.)

The other new model was the XL1200S, with S was for Sport. Same 1200 engine, all in natural alloy, cast 19- and 16-inch wheels, Dunlop Elite tires, with front and rear suspension tunable for damping as well as spring rate, and with dual front brakes. The wheels and brakes must be why the Sport weighed 15 pounds more than the Custom. These new models were in addition to the standard XLH1200, the deluxe 883, the Hugger 883 and the basic 883, making six versions of the same base model.

All the bases were covered. We aren't privy to the figures, but because the Softails were the best-selling family (then and now), it's safe to bet that the 1200C outsold the 1200S.

A historical note in that regard: Many chapters ago H-D's letter code was described if not deciphered. An L meant the second, tuned version, H was the next step, and so forth. Harley-Davidson's new owners changed the code. They did it by using letters that stood for something! Yes, indeed. There was the FXE, with E for electric, and the FLT, as in Touring, followed by the little-known XLT, the touring Sportster.

But now, for 1996, the lesser models kept the XLH, with the XLH883 and XLH1200, while the new offerings were the XL1200S and XL1200C.

It's an obscure point, but sometimes the little things are clues to what the company is doing and thinking. And surely they wanted to make things clearer.

In still another logical move—remember the adoption of belt drive?—all the Sportsters got the 3.3-gallon tank for 1997, while the cast wheels were redone with 13 spokes instead of the 7 and 9 spokes of earlier versions.

Harley-Davidson observed its 95th Anniversary in 1998 and of course there were special editions for all the model lines. The XL family observed the occasion with a limited edition 1200C, done in (quoting again) "Midnight Red and Champagne Pearl," and sold with a serialized nameplate.

Next came some fashion shifting, and some leveling of the curve.

Fashion first. Ever since the days of the staggered shorty dual mufflers that distinguished the early CH, small mufflers have been the hot ticket. (The English sportbikes had the same thing, by the way.)

In scientific fact, larger mufflers are better because they can reduce noise with less restriction of airflow.

The flat track tuners learned this years ago and fit silencers so big they're known as boom boxes.

But the street racers cared more for image than actual speed and insisted on small mufflers. The accessory guys learned quickly that you couldn't give efficient mufflers away if they didn't look the part. Keep that in mind because the performance news in 1998 was an upgraded edition of the 1200S.

It should have been named the XLCH1200. The sporting 1200 had benefited from its cousin the Buell, H-D's sports department.

The '98 Sport's compression ratio was raised from 9:1 to 10:1. It had a single-fire ignition, dual spark plugs, four coils, and a tailored advance curve. There were better camshafts and the suspension was tunable for damping as well as spring stiffness fore and aft. A Vance & Hines muffler was also an option. However, few buyers bothered.

As another quirk (or drawback), H-D corporate policy at the time downplayed facts like horsepower claims or ratings. Instead, the press release said the 1200 Sport had increased its average torque, the twisting force delivered at mid range, by 15 percent.

Motorcyclist magazine tested a '98 1200 Sport.

They were puzzled. While the factories were getting vague on claims, the magazines were becoming more precise. Could one have caused the other?

If so, *Motorcyclist* was checking test machines on a chassis dynamometer, and said that the '96 1200S they tested with the milder engine delivered 54.4 bhp to the pavement. The '98's peak output was an even 57 bhp. The Sport's best drag-strip time was 13.36 seconds, which is quick but a long way from a record and not much improvement on earlier XLs that hadn't received all that speed equipment.

That disappointment aside, the *Motorcylist* crew was impressed with the smooth power—torque surely was boosted as the factory claimed—and with the handling. They approved of the larger tank, but said the Sportster was something of a vibrator.

Was the new, tuned engine worse that it had been? Certainly not. Instead, what we're beginning to see is relativity. That is, the rival twins and the bigger Harleys were now so smooth that the XLs began to seem worse than they otherwise were.

Model years 1999 through 2001 were carryover years, well, for the Sportsters anyway. The Motor Company was busy with other projects, whole new models and families in fact, and the XLs were selling well enough to allow business as usual.

In 2002, there was a shift in the other direction.

We need to change focus here. The Sportster XL engines and the racing XR-750 engine became distant cousins 30 years before this. The XR-750 has defeated or outlasted its rivals since, right up to this minute.

But the American Motorcyclist Assn. divided the national championship into dirt track and road course titles, and H-D was out of the road race half for years.

Then in a debacle too painful to recount here, H-D commissioned a completely new road racing effort. None of the people in the new team had ever done any motorcycle racing. All the people in H-D's racing department, the chaps who'd dominated the dirt series for 20 years, were shut out.

Why? No one who knows will talk and those who will talk weren't in a position to know. Call it politics. Call it millions of dollars down the slippery slide.

Meanwhile, the AMA had created a dirt track and a road race series for Sportsters. And sure, H-D had a hand in the plan and the machines were taken from the showrooms, stripped, and rebuilt by hand so they were lots faster and lighter than the stock versions. But even so, the XL racers gave newcomers and dealers a chance to go racing and a good number did just that.

On the grounds that this gave new appeal to racing and sport, and to sort of cash in on the evergreen, OK, ever orange and black, XR-740, for 2002 the 883C was joined by the 883R.

This began with the basic 883, except it got a new, this-model-only, dual seat, wide and flat han-

Take your pick: custom or sport.

dlebars just like the dirt guys grip, the dual front brakes and cast wheels from the 1200S, a really sharp orange and black paint scheme, and a 2-into-1 exhaust system that came with a large, efficient muffler that sounded good, delivered power, and met the noise rules.

One could say this addition created the Sportster's extended family: the basic 883, the Hugger, the 883R and 883C, the optioned versions of the 1200 plus the 1200C and 1200R. The sports and cruiser models filled the market niches between the bargain 883s and the big twins plus V-Rod.

All this made sense and earned money for Harley-Davidson, especially in a booming motorcycle market.

It also made sense, therefore, for The Motor Company to keep the lineup as it was for 2003 ... but wait!

CHAPTER TEN

THE NEXT GENERATION: 2004 AND BEYOND

The 2004 R model features the familiar Sportster curves.

For 2004 the Sportster lineup went through its second revolution.

At this point in time and progress, readers who began at the beginning—as opposed to owners who skipped to admire their machines first—will be able to predict the next several paragraphs.

The Motor Company doesn't break the rules it makes. In the summer of 2003, the motorsports press was invited to a new model launch.

The start of the show was—you see how easy this is to guess?—a new Sportster.

Harley-Davidson's 2004 middleweight had . . . the 45-degree included angle, the air cooling, the fork-and-blade connecting rods, the primary drive on the left and output sprocket on the right, and the arc of four single-lobe camshafts first seen on the Model D of 1929.

Unit construction, telescopic fork front suspension and swinging arm rear suspension, introduced on the Model K of 1952.

Cassette style gearbox, from the KH of 1954.

Overhead valves, two per cylinder, as seen on the original Sportster of 1957.

A recognizable version of the 1966 Hamcan air cleaner. Oh, and the oil tank below the seat on the right, the staggered dual exhausts, the sprocket cover and gearcase cover with the housing for the ignition and what looked like the mount for a generator . . . enough of this. As H-D has been doing since 1929 at least, and has done because it worked and still does, the 2004 Sportster was virtually all new in every detail.

Its improvements came just in time, while in general and at a glance, genetics rule again.

Real (No Kidding) Rubber

Let's begin with the new. Harley-Davidson didn't invent the idea or do it first, but some engines—singles, most twins and triples, and some variety of fours—are inherently unbalanced. With one piston going up and down it's impossible to make it balance by spinning other parts 'round and 'round.

The narrow angle V-twin, especially one with two connecting rods sharing the single throw, as Harley engines have always done, is as inherently imbalanced as it's possible to be.

Back in the late 1970s (using AMF's money, it's fair to note), Harley engineers realized that if you couldn't eliminate the vibrations, you could isolate the forces that generated them. They designed a new frame, which kept the engine, gearbox, and final drive together. They mounted the entire power train with a system of flexible connections, so the motorcycle is two assemblies, with the drivetrain and rear suspension as one collection, and the frame, front end, handlebars, seat, tanks, and so forth the other collection. The two are connected via linkage and joints using a flexible material for bushings. The engine still vibrates, but now the rider and controls are isolated from the vibrations.

This system works. It worked for Harley's FLT models and for Norton's vertical twins—that's where Isolastic came from—and H-D expanded the idea with the FXR family, sporting smaller big twins with isolation mounts.

Moving in normal Motor Company deliberation, all the big touring models and the Dyna-Glides that followed the FXRs got the mounts.

For a technical tidbit here, know that FXR has always been presumed to stand for Super Glide plus Rubber, often quipped into Rubberglide . . . except that the flexible bushings were made of some sort of poly-

mer or synthetic, just as the raw material used in car and motorcycle tires is, and never mind being told to keep the rubber side down, there is no rubber side, except until 2004, for some truck tires.

Harley-Davidson's touring models got the isolation mounts and gained smoothness and comfort and durability and allowed use of the same engine configuration long after the critics predicted it was obsolete. Same goes for the same basic engine used in the Rubberglides and Dynaglides. (The exception at this writing has been the Softails, which used solid engine mounts first because the marketing staff decided Softail buyers want some vibration for tradition's sake. Plus, those folks don't ride that many miles and vibration isn't a problem for them. Later, as the market matured, H-D offered the big twin with counter-balancers, so the engine shakes less while being rigidly mounted in the frame.)

During the 20-plus years all the above was taking place, it's always been sort of assumed by followers of motorcycling that one day the Sportster would receive similar treatment.

No prize for knowing the day came in summer of 2003.

Working from the center out, the solidly mounted, unit construction, XL engine had served as a frame stiffener; a bulwark in effect. With the engine floating, well sort of, in the frame, torsional resistance was less.

There is an optimal stiffness to frame design, and the old frame, all steel or not, wasn't stiff enough. So the frame was beefed up. The package had to fit within the old parameter, don't forget, so the frame tubes were made thicker and got extra gusseting.

While the frame was being redesigned, the engineers took advantage of the opportunity and changed the frame section below the seat, the section that carries the seat, from a round tube to a flat stamping. The seat mounting was an inch lower, ditto the seat itself and thus the static ride height and, presto, there was no longer a need or excuse for the Hugger option.

Chief among changes to the new bikes was rubber mounting for the engines.

The '04 XL engine was radically changed, much more so than it looks, or the labels imply. There are two versions, an 883 and a 1200. Same bores and stroke as before, and as mentioned there are pushrods, air cooling, and two-valves-per-cylinder. And care was taken with such items as the gearcase cover styled to look like the mount for the generator, two generations after the generator was replaced with an alternator and the space filled by an oil filter.

The displacements are done for sales appeal. In contrast, the V-Rod engine is loosely based on the failed VR racing project. Except that the VR displaced 1,000 cc because that was the legal limit and the V-Rod designers wanted 115 bhp so they boosted the displacement to 1,100 cc because that was the size needed to meet that goal with a low stress state of tune.

In contrast, the XL engines' bores and strokes came first because, as the Motor Family's Bill Davidson has noted, the owners refer to their 883s or 1200s before they say "Sportster."

Step back a bit here. Harley-Davidson's cutting edge, the radical skunk works where new ideas can make end runs around corporate caution, is Buell, a brand that began when former H-D engineer Eric Buell bought surplus XR1000 engines to go racing, and which is now a mostly-owned H-D subsidiary.

Current Buells are powered by versions of XL engines, except that the Buell guys have improved and souped up the originals for extra power. They also did things like make a Buell 984 by keeping the 1200's 3.5 inch bore while de-stroking the engine from 3.8 to 3.13 inches. Along this path, they came out with new cylinder heads atop what was basically the XL cases.

So now, meanwhile, the Isolation XL had to have new cases because the engine mounts were very different and the swingarm was to mount on the back of the engine instead of the frame. This allowed H-D to use the new Buell cylinder heads, with better breathing

and a 9.7:1 compression ratio on the new lower end. All while looking like the old engine.

The cylinders have more finning, for more cooling, and the lubrication system has more capacity, 3.6 quarts instead of 3.0. With oil sprayed on the pistons, the engineers say their tests show 40 degrees cooler than the old engine under the same conditions. There are new rocker boxes, in two pieces rather than three, meaning two fewer gaskets and two fewer places to leak. One of the little flaws in the Evo XL engine was an occasional rocker box gasket failure.

Electronic ignition is retained, and so is the 40-mm Keihin carburetor, for both the 883 and the 1200. Davidson told *Cycle World* that the planners considered fuel injection but kept the carb because one, it's cheaper and keeps the bike's price down and two, Sportster owners like to tune, modify, and improve their engines. Swapping carburetors is heaps easier and cheaper than fiddling with EFI.

In that discussion, Davidson said judicious use of Screaming Eagle parts, as in less restriction to the intake and exhaust systems, would deliver 90 bhp at the rear wheel.

Camshift timing and general tune, in stock form, was done to deliver 1200 performance equal to the previous 1200 Sport model.

There's a serendipitous benefit with the exhaust system. Ever since the government mandated noise limits, XLs have come with an ugly balance tube between the two head pipes. (The factory has always said it's for power, so how come all racing engines use separate pipes, eh?)

The isolation mounting, though, uses two selectively stiff steel and rubber mounts below the engine and transmission.

Oh. Rubber. The mounts use real rubber, which for some reason worked best in tests. The drawback is that the Sportster is the only Harley without Glide in its name, so we finally have Rubber-non-Glides to go with the earlier non-Rubber-Glides (that's a joke).

But the isolation mounts—the flexible platforms and nonadjustable tie rods limiting engine movement to a vertical plane—prevent the exhaust system from bring mounted on the frame, as the pipes have been for as long as there have been mufflers.

The new XLs therefore have a cantilevered strut, running way back from the engine to the rear muffler. And while they were doing that component, the engineers added a cross-over tube, joining the two pipes invisibly just aft of the swingarm pivot, and the ugly tube has disappeared. Neat.

Again, in keeping with tradition, the really new isolation mounts and virtually new engine arrive in company with existing features, such as belt final drive, five forward speeds, disc brakes, and electronic ignition.

Fraternal Twins

With the two engine choices come two models on the same platform.

Traditionalists may take some offense here. The first two models that followed the original XL were the XLR, the track-ready TT racer, and the XLC, the stripper dirt bike requested by the California dealers.

Surely it's no coincidence that the '04 Sportster comes as either the XLR1200, the R meaning Roadster (a name tried once before don't forget), and the XLC1200, C meaning Custom.

For purists, this is like Ford using the legendary Cobra name on a four-cylinder tiddler with fancy paint. Or Ferrari tagging a road car, air-conditioned even, with the Testa Rossa moniker that ruled road courses a generation earlier.

Which is, of course, the point. You'd have to accost 1,000 current Harley riders before you'd find one who'd ever heard of an XLR or XLC. While the initials do apply to the names, never mind that the Roadster tag will disappear again because Sportster owners are proud to own Sportsters.

That gripe aside, the XLR is the basic Sportster, the model designed to follow tradition. It's got the 3.3-

gallon tank, the cast 19- and 16-inch wheels, paint that mimics the early '60s XLCH, low bars. Even a head-light mounted on an eyebrow, as seen on the street-legal XLCH of 1959. There are updates, as in a wider rear tire than the '03 Sport used. And there's a real fork lock (although there's still is no toolkit or helmet lock. Perhaps someday . . .).

The XLC is a mild Custom. As mentioned, the seat is lower and the shocks are 1.5 inches shorter. The controls are further forward and the bars are drag-style, flat, and mounted on what the chopper guys call dog-bone risers.

The fuel tank is sculpted, with a full 4.5-gallon capacity, and it looks like the swoopy tanks done by the custom (lower case here) shops, or H-D's own Dyna models (the ruder guys in the press corps instantly nicknamed the XLC the Dynette, the junior version of the Super Glide).

The XLC has the now-classic 21-inch front wheel, spoked. The rear wheel is a slotted disc, also with a wider rear tire.

The 2004 Custom retained the model's classic looks, and got real rubber to separate the riders from the vibrations.

The S model was dropped for 2004; the Roadster version shown here carried the performance torch.

Both models use Showa suspension front and rear, and Nissin disc brakes (a change of supplier).

How They Work

The measure of Harley-Davidson's success with the new Sportster can begin with a true story.

Cycle World introduced the new models in September 2003. The timing here was crucial. The magazine was in on the secret early. They had to be because it takes months to get a magazine story into print. The *CW* staff was riding the XLR and XLC for testing and photography weeks before the public knew about the new Sportster.

At this same time, The Motor Company was celebrating its 100th year, with the big party mentioned earlier. *Cycle World* organized a ride to the party, with readers from across the U.S. and Europe.

The group assembled at *Cycle World*'s office and shop and toured the place. Ready? Parked in *Cycle World*'s shop were an XLR and an XLC, the very machines used in the test. The guests, all Harley riders naturally, all experienced guys with years of riding and looking . . . walked right past the new XLs. One even liked the paint and the tank on the XLC.

The C model was the only Sportster to not use the traditional eyebrow headlight mount. The R model retained it for 2004.

The C model continued to keep it simple.

The 21-inch front wheel on the C still said "cruiser."

But no one spotted the secret bikes.

Harley-Davidson's execs and planners wanted to keep the traditional look? No worries, mates. The bad news, oddly enough, comes with the objective figures.

For the Sportster's first 45-plus years, the bike's weight usually tipped the scales at just barely under 500 pounds. The test weights varied, as in dry or wet, how much equipment and so forth, or if the testers did the full job or relied on the factory's claims. But the reports ranged from 485 to 501, OK?

Cycle World weighed its test XLR and came up with a certified dry-tank weight of 559 pounds. Add fuel and it was 579 pounds.

Factory engineers predicted this when they said the new frame would add 50 or so pounds to the total. But even so, that's close to 100 pounds more than the original XL, even allowing for different test procedures. And it's close to the average weight of a Super Glide, the next step up Harley's ladder.

Back with the good news, the designers aimed to have the new 1200 equal the earlier 1200 Sport. And the XLR turned the quarter-mile in 13.25 seconds, against the 13.36 from *Motorcyclist*'s test.

If there's a price for the added weight it was that the XLR's mileage averaged 41 mpg, a bit less than reported for older 1200s and a lot less than the high 50s from the Evo 883s.

The bottom line: the pay-off here has to be . . . does the isolation system work?

Yes.

There's no question about that.

The details are more complicated. We've seen that the perception of vibration and the reports as to how much it matters varies with circumstances.

Any motorized vehicle has some vibration. As the Greek philosophers used to teach, you can cut something in half, and in half again, and again and again, but although what you have gets smaller and smaller, you always have something.

Not only that, but when the new XLs were being designed and the mounting system tested and compared with the big twin, Buell, and other similar systems, it was all done with the understanding that motorcycles need some vibration, some pulsing and noise, some action.

The point?

Nobody's ever going to push the start button of an ISO-XL when the engine's already running. The engine and drivetrain vibrate, move around visibly, just as they do with a Buell, Super Glide, or Norton Commando. Under normal operating conditions, the occupied portions of the motorcycle, and thus the occupants, are in fact isolated from the worst of the shakes and buzzing.

The whole package is improved. Clutch pull is reduced, shifts are cleaner, quieter, and lighter. The mounting system has been tuned and the sweet spot, as racers say, includes almost all of the engine's usable rev band, from 2,000 to 5,000 rpm.

Lug it or buzz it, and it will shake or vibrate. But of course Sportster owners are mechanically inclined and empathize with their machines, or they won't be Sportster owners for very long.

Within that useful rev band, the engine hums, the smaller grips are calm, and the images in the mirrors are clear.

Cycle World's testers and reporters are sports or hardcore guys, with lots of saddle time. So it made sense for them to report that the XLR is an all day motorcycle, sharp and suited to life in top gear.

The XLC, they said, is just as fast and just as good technically, but the forward mounts and slouching posture are tiring on the highway if stylish at the watering hole. The front wheel flops in tight turns, which is part of the custom manner, no big deal.

Meanwhile, the XLC has the same powertrain as the XLR and by extension will deliver the same speed and performance and durability.

Summaries Long and Short

This is a point that probably should have been made several hundred pages earlier, but . . .

This is not a history of the Harley-Davidson Sportster. This is a history of the Sportster to date.

To contrast with a contemporary, the VW Beetle has a history. It begins in the 1930s, with versions of the fabled car fairly close to what became famous and ends, if memory serves, in 2003 when the last versions of the VW derived package went out of production.

That's the contrast. The latest (or current, depending on when this is being read) Sportsters are just going into production.

The engine was all new, but still recognizably an XL engine.

The rubbermount XL's primary drive cover is new and completely different, but retains the overall look and purpose first seen in the 1952 Model K.

Odds are tradition will continue and in a model year or two there will be a touring version, a full sports option, a more extreme custom, maybe even a Hugger revival.

Next, keep in mind that the Sportster has never been the starter model, not for The Motor Company.

In 1957, when the first XL arrived, H-D offered the two-stroke single Hummer, followed by the four-stroke Sprints.

In showrooms for 2004, next to the XLs, are Buell Blasts, single-cylinder four-strokes derived from the XL engine.

Sad to say, Harley-Davidson has always been more willing to offer the public new and different bikes than the public has been willing to buy them.

What this has meant in the long run, aside from some excellent machines not selling as they deserved to sell, is that the Sportster has always been the company's middleweight.

Another major gene in The Motor Company's genome is that H-D has always been market-driven. Sure, the critics have scoffed. They've also made fun of General Motors, especially when GM had 60-plus percent of the American market.

But quoting John R. Bond, the man who made *Road & Track* the standard of the motoring journal world, "General Motors does an excellent job designing cars for the people who buy them."

Harley-Davidson still does just that, witness a century in business. If the market wants bigger starter bikes and larger middleweights, that's what H-D will provide.

What we've seen here is the first 46 years of Sportster history.

What we'll see next . . . well heck, more Sportsters, what else?

It is the best name in motorcycling.

It's still air-cooled, it still uses pushrods, and the XL engine still gets the job done.

INDEX